ALSO BY BJÖRGVIN BENEDIKTSSON

Better Mixes in Less Time:
The Productivity Playbook for Mixing Engineers

Get More Gigs: The Essential Guide To Booking,
Performing And Making Money From Gigs As An
Independent Musician

How to Record Great Music...with whatever equipment
you got

Step By Step Mixing:
How to Create Great Mixes Using Only 5 Plug-ins

Workbooks with bundled video courses
by Björgvin Benediktsson

EQ Strategies: Your Ultimate Guide to EQ

Drum Mix Toolkit: Kick the Habit of Crappy Home Studio
Drums

Expert Home Vocals: How to Produce Quality Vocals From
Your Project Studio

Find out more about these books and courses at
www.audio-issues.com

YOU GET WHAT YOU GIVE

A Simple Story for Finding Success in the Music Business

BJÖRGVIN BENEDIKTSSON

Paperback ISBN: 978-1-7336888-3-3

Published by Björgvin Benediktsson & Audio Issues. Tucson, Arizona

More about this book and additional resources can be found at www.YouGetWhatYouGiveBook.com

TABLE OF
CONTENTS

INTRODUCTION I

CHAPTER 1
Take This Job and Shove It 9

CHAPTER 2
If a Website Goes Up, Does Anybody Care? 19

CHAPTER 3
Stairway, Denied. 33

CHAPTER 4
A Man of Routine 39

CHAPTER 5
What Got You Here Won't Get You There 47

CHAPTER 6
Creativity in the Kitchen 67

CHAPTER 7
Taking Care of Business 75

CHAPTER 8
What's Their Problem?! 81

CHAPTER 9
Success Likely 95

CHAPTER 10
Imposter Syndrome 103

CHAPTER 11
Who's Your Friend? 117

CHAPTER 12
Which Package Would You Like? 135

CHAPTER 13
Putting it Together 145

EPILOGUE
Somebody Loan Me a Dime 151

THANK YOU 157

ACKNOWLEDGEMENTS 159

ABOUT THE AUTHOR 161

To Lilja Sif
I can't wait to help you make an impact.

INTRODUCTION

How do you become a successful six figure business in a music industry that never seems to end its decline? For me, it started with €0.34.

Back in 2009, in the stone-age years of the internet, I had been writing my little audio blog for a few months, publishing what I was learning as an audio engineering student at the SAE Institute campus in Madrid. On the side, I had enrolled in an "online business" course and one of their income-generating strategies was to earn money from Google ads. This sounded promising to me - so I added some to my site. Then I waited. Alone in my dimly lit basement apartment, I refreshed the Google Ads dashboard waiting for the big clicks to come in.

All I got were crickets. Either that, or the cockroach infestation of my apartment was getting worse. After what felt like a billion data packets later, somebody clicked an ad on my site and it made me a whopping €0.34! So, I did what any short-term thinking college student would do and I went out on the town to celebrate my online riches, probably spending a hundred times more in food and drinks than I earned in income. I quickly learned that selling advertising was a losing business strategy if you wanted to run a sustainable business, but the thrill of earning money from your own online asset was a feeling like no other. I also learned the importance of celebrating the small wins that give you momentum to move onto bigger challenges.

It's over a decade later. My business has grown from an ugly looking blog earning less than a dollar to a reputable audio education platform earning more than six figures per year. And to think it all started because of one moment when a random person clicked on my Google ad, earning me a measly €0.34! Every big endeavor starts small and snowballs from there. As the Bill Hicks joke goes: you can't learn to fly if you don't take off from the ground first, no matter how much acid you take. Small wins are the guideposts along the way as you scale the mountain of your success.

I believe good business starts with the mindset of making something you're proud of. Making an impact and creating a lasting body of work that lives without you is a mission that someone who races to the bottom of the discount pile and cuts corners instead of committing to quality will never achieve. What you will find in the following pages are some of the most important lessons I've learned from growing a successful business in the music industry. We'll follow Casey's story as he learns the mindset behind making an impact in his career, from the importance of routine and the power of value-based pricing, to understanding his clients and diversifying his income streams. I've found these lessons to be the core building blocks of a sustainable business and now you will have the opportunity to implement them in yours to grow your career. Along the way, we will pause to consider the various mindsets you must have to make an impact with your own career. These little Success Strategies break up the chapters and are a chance for you to reflect on how you would implement what Casey is learning in your own life. For those of you wanting to learn even more than what these pages include, I have put together additional resources and worksheets for you to use in your journey at www.YouGetWhatYouGiveBook.com.

Traditional business wisdom tells you to find a niche because the "riches are in the niches." Similarly, comedy tells you to be specific because it elevates the joke to another level. So, in order for me to write a business book that was similar to the business parables I so enjoyed, I had to set it in a world I was familiar with. Having run Audio Issues as a successful online business in the music industry for ten years meant that I had a lot of experience in a very narrow niche, yet the business principles I share in this book can be used across industries and disciplines.

This book came to be because of an offhand remark by my friend Chris Graham of the Six Figure Studio Podcast. He joked on our mastermind call that my next book should be a business parable for the recording engineer. Unbeknownst to him, I had been wanting to write a "how-to fiction parable" for a while, with thousands of words of unpublished ideas, scenes, and dialog that I wasn't sure what to do with. His request came at the right time and his idea gave me the structure I needed to get started. The first bullet-point draft poured out of me over the course of a few days, later expanding into a standard zero to hero story arc. Then COVID came and it gave me time to expand on the draft and give it a different feel than the traditional business parables we were used to. If I was writing for the music industry, the book had to be a little more Rock 'n' Roll than Suit & Tie. So, as with every creative endeavor, it started somewhere and then morphed along the way into something unrecognizable from its original inspiration. If good artists borrow and great artists steal, it's because great artists are also obsessed with hiding their theft in such a way that their originality wipes out the origin of their inspiration.

I, like any other creative I've known about: obscure, unknown or renowned, suffer from imposter syndrome and it's never been more apparent than in the writing of this introduction. I'm dealing with imposter syndrome and procrastination as I'm writing this because I know that when I finish the introduction, which one should leave until the end, the book is ready for release. And when you release something you have to let it go. You have to give it up and hope for the best. At best, you'll get accolades for your art. At worst, the sharks will circle and rip you into the abyss, leaving you awful reviews with ad hominem attacks.

However, in reality, chances are you'll get a bit of both. Life is nothing if not about balance and like the author David Leddick taught me a long time ago through his book, *I'm Not for Everyone. Neither are You*, you will never be liked by everyone who comes across your work. If being a writer and educator in the audio industry has taught me anything it's that there are plenty of people (mostly men) that are ready to rip you apart and feel superior just to feed their disguised jealousy. But if you have the tenacity to move past the attacks and focus on the ones you can help, you'll learn that there are plenty of people (men and women), who are eager to enrich and improve their lives by listening to what you have to say. I believe the world is a better place if you meet people where they are, seek to understand their problems and help them make an impact. This is one of the core tenets of Noah's teachings in this book you are now reading, and it's my hope that you will take those ideals into consideration when making an impact with your business.

If there's one thing that my business has given me above all else it's the freedom to design the lifestyle I want without asking for anybody's permission. Permission is a weird construct that creatives can often feel jailed by. We worry about whether our art is good enough and whether we have any right to lean into our inspirations and create the things we feel inside. Whatever you're working on when this book happens to cross your path, remember this: You don't need permission to build something you believe in. You don't need permission to run things your way as long as it gives you what you want. There is no one way to have a successful career. You don't need permission to mix two disparate ideas together and create something new, however crazy it sounds. That's literally the definition of innovation. You don't need permission to start your own thing. There are no gatekeepers. You don't need permission. Your creativity is the permission you need to create. Just promise me you'll let it out into the world and give other people permission to experience it. Your creativity can make an impact on your future, you only have to believe in it. To paraphrase Lt. Colonel Frank Slade, "Don't destroy it. Protect it. Embrace it. It's gonna make you proud one day, I promise you."

Of all the books I've written, this one was the hardest so far. The first draft whizzed by as a fun exercise. Then the rewriting started and the closer I got to the finish line the slower I worked and the harder it was to overcome the self-doubt of whether it was worth the effort of publishing. It's funny, the entire mission of my business is to encourage musicians to overcome their fears about releasing their music into the world. So if anything, it's been an interesting, although hypocritical exercise in "do as I say, not as I do," as I've worked to push past my own limiting beliefs about my own value in the world. In a word, it's taken a lot of willpower to put this book out. Yet here we are.

This book was hard to write because these limiting beliefs don't go away. You have to fight them every day. Writing this book pushed me out of my comfort zone because it was a stark contrast to the how-to books I'm used to writing. I could've easily chosen a different topic and kept to my regular voice. But I was so inspired by the parables that came before that I decided that I did in fact have the gall to write something similar.

Imposter syndrome would ask, who are you to write such a thing? Who gave you permission to venture off your beaten path? Please stick to the rivers and the lakes that you're used to!

Yet I dared into the arena with the other men and women who put their creativity on the line, ready for the one-star reviews and the pummeling of the internet trolls. If the worst thing to happen is a one-star review and indifference, this book will still tower as a trophy on my bookshelf. A reminder that I ignored the insecurities, pushed past my comfort zone and gave myself the permission to conquer my inner critic. It's my hope that this inspires you to do the same, no matter what type of creative you are. Let this short story about marketing, music, and making an impact be the inspiration you need to forge a path up your own mountain of success and find your own small wins along the way.

Björgvin Benediktsson

August 27th, 2020

CHAPTER 1

TAKE THIS JOB AND SHOVE IT

The wall clock of the office crashed into the next minute with a cathedral-style reverb. *K-Chunk!* It echoed in Casey's mind, but none of his coworkers seemed to notice. He made his rounds, noise-canceling headphones on his head playing a combination of the sort of music that tells others to leave you alone and let you do your job. Trent Reznor growled "Every Day is Exactly the Same" into Casey's headphones. The job was the furthest away from the dream he had when he enrolled in audio school, but earning a full-time income at a recording studio was a pipe-dream. The audio school administrators were eager to enroll you and take your money so that you could "follow your passion," but when classes were over, the harsh reality of an oversaturated and underpaying industry showed its face.

The only job Casey could find, because at least his degree fell into the *technology* category, was in IT. His job was a random collection of tech tasks that nobody else seemed competent to do, no matter how easy they were. It was as if management had come together one day to create a department for no other reason than it being an excuse to have a meeting.

Casey imagined the VP asking, "Right, where should we put X, Y, and Z?"

"Put it under IT?" a junior VP asked.

"Fantastic! Give this guy a promotion. What's for lunch?"

And that's how Casey got a job at Oasis Online Ops. Oasis Online Ops was one of those companies that helped internet marketers create misleading ads that got unsuspecting social media scrollers to join a webinar. The webinar would promise the world and sell these hapless internetizens on the dream of working four hours a week as an internet guru.

"Work from the Beach!" the clickbait beckoned.

"The office for today!" the Instagram caption exclaimed, the image showing a laptop sitting underneath an umbrella. Never mind the fact that it's impossible to work from the beach. The sun's too bright. It glares at your computer screen, angry at your audacity to work on such a beautiful day. And let's not get started on the sand. It gets everywhere! The reason you go to the beach is for a vacation, not to find a new place to send emails and schedule meetings. But selling the dream was the name of their game and they had an entire stock photo department solely focused on taking pictures of beautiful people smiling in desirable locations. It was a Mirage Maker. A Funnel Filler.

Let's be honest: marketing is a mirage. The agency did everything for anybody who would pay and therefore did nothing well except earn money from organizations too dumb to know which half of their ad budget actually worked. The only thing that mattered was the recurring revenue from their clients. The average client didn't know any better so they paid exorbitant fees for immature marketers barely out of college, who cited their click-through rates, CPAs and best marketing practices with Dunning-Kruger-like stupidity, believing that they *all* were at least 100% smarter than the average bear.

"We're getting industry-standard results," the lanky 22-year-old account execs in oversized dress shirts told their clients while pointing at graphs that made them look sophisticated. *Look at how much time we put into the slide deck!* their youthful enthusiasm screamed on the inside. The clients nodded their heads in agreement, as if being in the middle of the bell curve was something to be proud of. Their clean-shaven baby faces would continue through the slide deck to showcase just how much work they had done in the previous month, while their five-figure invoice was simultaneously emailed to their accounting department, continuing the charade for another billing cycle.

The Karens couldn't go a day without accidentally uninstalling important programs from their computers and Casey wasn't sure how long he could keep it up.

There were only so many times one could ask a college-educated adult whether they had turned it off and on again, and he was closing in on his 10,000th. He hoped he could spend the next 10,000 hours on something more valuable.

Yes, he could reset their password. Yes, he could change their log-in permissions for the new computer. No, he wouldn't get them coffee.

He had become complacent over the years. The job was a curse with a steady paycheck which he used to pour into his hobby of recording. Mics, pre-amps, fancy monitoring systems. He even splurged on acoustic treatment for his room so he could actually hear what was coming out of his speakers. He was a gifted songwriter and multi-instrumentalist and he'd learned enough about production to be dangerous, but he said goodbye to that dream every time he left for the office.

Yes, he could update their drivers. Yes, he could send the technical specs over to Development. No, he couldn't delete their browser history.

The only thing lacking from his taking the metaphorical leap through the fifteenth-floor window into freedom was, ironically, his lack of marketing knowledge to find clients to make his side-hustle a steady gig. Turned out that a degree from the land of Audio did very little to prepare him for the real world.

He was stuck in his dead-end job and he knew that the only way he could quit was a constant stream of clients into his home studio. However, by powers out of his control, his need for clients was fast-tracked the following Friday. At lunch the company sent out a memo to all of their employees.

From: MGMT

To: Everybody

To our valued employees:

Due to recent changes in our organizational structure, we are in need of some unfortunate restructuring of our staff. Starting this afternoon, we will have to lay off 20% of our workforce. Please take the rest of Friday off and wait for further communication at the end of the day.

Sincerely,

Management

Valued employees my ass. That was the most impersonal memo he'd seen from management yet, and it lit a fire inside of him. He slumped in his desk chair, rolled his eyes and sighed. "Ticks and Leeches" by Tool blared into his ears at a dangerously loud decibel level. Casey had no interest in spending the rest of the day worried about whether or not he had a job. Was management really this impersonal that they would hang a whole afternoon over their employees' heads until they let them know whether they had a job?

It was time to rip the cord out of the socket and tie a noose around his job. If he was ever going to have a career he enjoyed, he had to quit the job he hated. He stormed into the boss's office. His boss hunched over his computer, wearing the standard white dress-shirt of the corporate tribe, eyes mindlessly reading the screen in front of him while nibbling on a sandwich that was dangerously close to falling apart onto his keyboard.

"I quit. Effective immediately. Thank you for the employment so far but I'm needed elsewhere." His boss broke out of his stupor, stunned by Casey's words. A tomato slid out his sandwich and smeared his shirt with the saliva-like liquid and mayo, reminding Casey of the cover to Metallica's "Reload." He vanished from the office before his former boss could react, packed up his things and left.

No, he couldn't attend the mandatory training. No, he couldn't set up the projector. Yes, he could leave and never come back.

As Casey walked to his car, the furious scat-jazz of "Step Right Up" by Tom Waits blared out of a red convertible that zoomed down the street and rounded the corner.

The panic attacked Casey from the inside, like he was carrying a parasitic anaconda to term, a type of pregnancy that was squeezing his organs so hard he couldn't breathe. The only bright side of quitting on a

Friday was that he could use the weekend to hyperventilate into a paper bag. He relived the memory of quitting his job with a mixture of regret and pride. He knew he did the right thing by quitting his job. He wasn't going to last much longer anyway. It was only a matter of time before he would explode with rage at another company toe-touch.

He couldn't imagine himself becoming just another employee forever. Another cog in the system wasn't the passion he wanted to follow. He collapsed into his chair and felt the walls of his home recording studio closing in, pearls dripping down his forehead and sweat gushing from his armpits. His steady employment had afforded him the cash to put together a state-of-the-art recording facility in his converted garage. It wasn't a giant commercial facility, but it was big enough to fit a band and he had all the necessary equipment to make great music.

He surveyed his studio: Three sets of monitors stared at him, his desk chair creating an equilateral triangle. He had 12 lines of microphone inputs, an 88-key midi-controller, and various solid-state and tube amps, in addition to the rack-mounted amp modeler installed in his studio desk. Fancy microphones sat stacked in their cases on the shelf. The more expensive ones tucked away in the closet. Acoustic treatment hung in the early reflection zones and diffusers covered the back wall. His computer was fast enough to power an army of Apollo rockets to the moon, while simultaneously mixing a film-score, a rock opera and a symphony orchestra. But the equipment wasn't enough. Gear was useless if there was nobody around to use it. He needed to look for a job, or figure out how to make a business out of his studio. The lack of security terrified him, but as he looked around the studio, he felt a sense of exhilaration come over him. *This is it. I have to make this work.*

Yes, he would run a studio business. Yes, he would get clients. No, he had no idea where to start.

Music is a vehicle for emotion and Casey used it to coax the emotions needed to elevate his mood: Excitement, anger, sadness or, in this case, encouragement.

"Alexa, play my WinList," Casey commanded. From arguably the worst speaker housed in his studio, the room filled with the differences in sound pressure bouncing through the air, reflecting off the walls and echoing into his ears.

He brainstormed his next steps while the songs played: "Lose Yourself" by Eminem, "Stronger" by Kanye West, "All I Do is Win" by DJ Khalid, and of course, "My Shot" by Lin-Manuel Miranda. The music transformed his mood and he had stopped sweating, but his questions about business multiplied by the minute. He still had no idea how to get his studio started. How would he get clients? How should he promote his studio? How was he supposed to promote his studio without any music to showcase his work? Did he need a website? Should he start working for free to create a portfolio? Everything he Googled led to the same dead end. "Register for Our Webinar and You'll

Get Clients in No Time!" one page trumpeted, like a tap-dancing carnival barker lying through his teeth. Another page promised "Instant Results to Increase Your Revenue" and Casey felt like he was trapped in some kind of nightmare online version of The Music Man. *Ya got trouble all right.* Right here in the home studio.

No, he wouldn't register for the webinar. No, he wouldn't *Click Here to Get the Checklist!* Yes, he would continue looking.

He spent the weekend frantically Googling, but all he got were contradicting answers and convoluted business advice that didn't help with his particular situation. The only thing that seemed to be consistent was that future clients would want to see a portfolio of past projects.

The upside of his previous employment was his understanding of creating a bare-bones website. If he hoped to gain clients online, he'd need a website to house his portfolio. Over the weekend he threw up a one-page website from one of those flashy landing page templates he used to loathe so much. *I guess it's different if you believe in what you're selling,* Casey thought and shrugged. He even came up with a catchy name: *Casey Tones,* a play on his name and an homage to both the Grateful Dead and the hockey hooligan from Teenage Mutant Ninja Turtles. *Available for music production,* the website read.

And then he waited for the bands to show up.

CHAPTER 2
IF A WEBSITE GOES UP, DOES ANYBODY CARE?

C asey's mind was racing at a neurotic pace. Although an energetic 168 BPM was a recipe for an upbeat record, it was wildly unsustainable as a heart rate. It turned out that throwing up a website and telling the universe that you're open for business doesn't send a stream of clients your way.

The fluorescent lights of the coworking space buzzed at a constant 120 Hz and the anxiety slowly tightened around his esophagus like a vise. He couldn't take the isolation of his empty recording studio so he spent his afternoons here, if only for the occasional chat with nearby non-coworkers, a sliver of socialization looking more rare by the minute.

After rage-quitting his job the week before, he had spent the majority of his time frantically emailing every musical artist he could find online. He checked his bank account. Less than $3,000. Maybe he should've saved some money instead of buying all that gear that was now collecting dust instead of dividends. He'd need a steady stream of clients within a month or he was toast. Four weeks or he'd have to crawl back to the marketing agency with his tail between his legs begging for his job back. He inhaled with regret, kicking himself for spending so much money on equipment that wasn't getting used.

11 articles read. Create content, they all said, whatever that meant. 7 emails sent to potential bands. One Instagram feed post on a brand-new studio account that had no followers. 4 stories posted that nobody saw. Five fake smiles photographed around his gear uploaded to his website. A derailed argument on social media about which Metallica song was better: Master of Puppets or One. Casey made the mistake of commenting his intellectual argument on a social media post but forgot the fact that a lofty debate about the inherent meaning and storytelling aspects of a thrash metal song were going to be about as effective as making the case for dynamics if you were the mastering engineer behind "Death Magnetic." Casey stopped short of a flame war and exited stage left from social media with a swift thumb and middle finger on CMD+W.

Finally, feeling the early stage symptoms of carpal tunnel syndrome from what felt like hundreds of cold-emails, he got a reply from a rock band looking to record a demo. Trailer Trash Tendencies wasn't the most encouraging band name to get a reply back from, but beggars can't be choosers. This was it. This was his chance to get started and make a name for himself. He emailed back and forth with the frontman who told him, "We're totally looking to record something dude. We're playing tonight at the Old Dock. Come check us out!"

The Old Dock was a strange name for a landlocked bar in the middle of town. It was the type of venue that was continuously going out of business because running a venue where the main draw was one no-name underground band after another was a terrible business model.

Casey nodded to the doorman, who waved him through after checking his name on the list. Inside, he flashed the rock-on hand signal to the in-house engineer who had gotten him on the list and traded five bucks for a beer at the bar. $2,995 until it's time to crawl back to corporate America.

Black walls engulfed the performers and the audience. Stale beer and sweat lingered permanently in the air. Everywhere Casey stepped was sticky. It was the type of place that the Insane Clown Posse would stop on their tour, spray the Juggalos and the rest of the bar with their rider-demanded 400 two-liter bottles of Diet Faygo and leave for the next tour stop, but not before selling thousands of dollars in merch. Even though the staff lined the entire venue with throw-away carpet to absorb the root beer, the entire venue still needed deep-cleaning every time. It wasn't surprising that it was the only place where Trailer Trash Tendencies could get a gig.

They put on a good show, but they weren't the tightest band Casey had seen live. They sounded like a mix of grunge, synth-rock, and pop-punk, minus the cool guitar playing and infectious energy more proficient bands of any of those genres would give you live. They wore the obligatory torn jeans, sneakers and black t-shirts, with some band members opting for the sleeveless variety to air out the armpits. Casey sighed as he sipped his beer at the back of the venue, avoiding the mosh pit at the front of the stage. *You gotta start somewhere.* Casey wasn't a seasoned veteran of the industry. He wasn't filling any Lord-Alge shoes anytime soon. All he needed was a starting point and he'd take whatever he could get.

After their set, Casey slid through the crowd to the front of the stage where the band was packing up. Throngs of black t-shirts with illegible metalcore band names paid him no attention as they worked their hazy eyes and THC-laced brains out the door and into the night. Casey introduced himself and struck up a conversation with the band about their demo. The band wanted a raw sound and wanted it done live.

"Four hours," Jamie, the frontman said. "Weekends are best," he added.

They weren't selling out stadiums and swapping their day jobs for the rockstar lifestyle anytime soon, so they were limited to the weekends. Four hours was stretching it for a single. Although the band had played an entertaining show to the audience, Casey didn't feel they had the tightness they'd need to pull off a live recording. Inside his brain, the Time Management Molecule raised a red flag that was quickly shot down by the army of Overzealous Cells. He agreed, desperate for the money, the experience and the exposure.

"So, what's this gonna cost us?" Jamie asked, caressing his microphone, treating it like an extension of his body instead of an amplification of his voice.

Casey hesitated. Jamie's eyes narrowed down to slits and Casey's skin crawled. What was up with this guy? Casey hadn't thought about price at all. He came to the show to get to know them and hadn't anticipated getting down to business so quickly. He thought about putting prices on his website when he put it up, but he honestly had no idea how to price himself. He had a salary at the marketing agency so he had no clue where to start. It felt difficult to price something he would gladly do for free, but he knew he couldn't make a living that way.

He blurted out in a panic, "Let me run the numbers and get back to you tomorrow." Jamie rolled his eyes and shrugged as he proceeded to pack up the rest of his gear.

"Ok, guess I'll hear from you tomorrow," Jamie said while rolling up a mic cable.

"Sounds good," Casey said, gave the band a thumbs up and left.

On the way home Casey cursed himself. He repeated the scene in his head over and over. Should he have been better prepared? Should he have figured out his rate before going to the show? His face reflected on the dark windshield as he sped home in a fuss, lampposts zooming by like a four-on-the-floor beat. He gave himself the same lame thumbs up he had given the band at the end of their meeting, rolling his eyes and snorting at his naivety. He couldn't have loathed himself more, but then "Loser" by Beck came on the radio and that's how much that feeling escalated. He could still smell the lingering stench of sweat and beer and he hoped the cops would leave him alone. There was no way they wouldn't use the opportunity for a sobriety test. So stupid. He should've been better prepared. He still had no idea how to price himself so once he got home, he texted his friend Jen for advice.

Jen was a seasoned computer programmer who ran a successful freelance business setting up web apps for companies. She was bound to know something about figuring out how to price yourself, even if they weren't in the same industry. Jen told Casey that he should figure out an hourly rate that he would be happy with.

"Obviously rates can be all over the place depending on experience and education. A good place to start would be to find the median household income. That way you have a ballpark for standard of living in the city," Jen told him.

Casey figured that the median household income in his city was about $50,000 a year and if he wanted to give himself four weeks of vacation each year, he needed to make $26.04/hour. Even if he was working

40 hours/week, it was unrealistic to be able to bill for all of those hours because they would include administrative work and things that he couldn't charge clients for. Casey sighed and slumped down in his studio chair. He still wasn't anywhere close to figuring out a good price, but since he was just starting out, he settled on a flat $25/hour. If he stayed booked at the studio, he'd make enough money to get by, although it was a far cry from the success he desired. He could always raise his rates later, he hoped.

The next day he emailed his rate over to Jamie and the band to set a recording date for the following weekend.

"We only have a budget of $100 so that should work for us," Jamie emailed back, repeating his confidence in being able to record their demo so quickly. They agreed to a four-hour slot that Saturday and Casey felt exhilarated about getting his first band into the studio.

Casey got to work preparing his studio space ready for the band to show up. A full band recording had a lot of moving pieces so he wanted to be prepared and give off a good impression. Luckily, he had all the equipment he needed and although his studio wasn't the biggest, it sounded tight because of his strategically placed acoustic treatment. He line-checked the microphones. Tap, tap. The signal was weak but he figured the difference between a soft tap and a smashing thud would make up for the difference in level. He tapped the rest of the drum mics and the signal ran beautifully through the XLR cables into his preamps, shooting up through the faders of his interface in glowing green colors. He looked at his available outputs and counted. Kick drum, snare drum, probably two toms (he recalled from their set), a pair of overhead mics and a room mic. That was seven, so he could patch their bass player into a DI and isolate the two guitar amps in the other room, making room for Jamie's synth and a scratch vocal that would later get replaced.

When Saturday arrived, Casey was prepped and ready, but the band was anything but that. The recording session was a nightmare. The band showed up hungover and unprepared, indifferent about how that would impact their performance. They didn't waste any time cracking open a breakfast beer to make them feel better.

The drummer had red-light fever so as soon as Casey hit record he immediately started messing up, his proficiency as a drummer dropping several experience levels. He refused the click-track so he couldn't play in time and he kept dropping sticks because of his sweaty palms. Needless to say, the drum recording was all over the place.

After a particularly erratic performance, the drummer simply said, "I think that's good enough. Can't you just edit it so that it's tighter? Isn't that what you do?"

Casey told him, "Yes, it was possible to edit the drum tracks, but we should still get as tight of a recording as we can."

Casey weighed his options, knowing that at best he

would be polishing a turd. The drummer couldn't play in the pocket so he considered editing the entire performance to force the drum tracks onto the grid, but that would kill the groove. Fitting a human being into a quantized grid would make him sound technically perfect, but devoid of all feel.

He knew that if he chose that option, he would have to edit the drum tracks before recording anything else. Nothing kills a feel faster than a sloppy drum track made worse by instruments haphazardly recorded on top of a terribly out-of-time track. His other two options didn't promise much more; he could send the drummer home to practice or replace him with a proficient player. Casey didn't feel confident in the power moves of more established producers so all he was left with was patience and a ticking clock that was bound to go over the $100 budget.

After a few more takes, they had a decent drum track. Not a spectacular, in-the-pocket groove that mesmerized you in its consistency and drove you to the dance floor. Not the pile-driving performance of Josh Freese or the technically proficient percussion of Steve Gadd, but enough to keep the session going.

He sent the band to lunch while he edited the drum tracks with meticulous accuracy.

After lunch he proceeded with the overdubs. The rest of the band wasn't much better. The bass player continuously forgot to tune his bass, the guitar players had an awful, scooped-mid tone that didn't fit the sound of the song at all, and Jamie...well, Jamie was an egomaniac living inside a sack of shit with a cocaine problem. His frequent bathroom breaks did not escape Casey's attention and at one point, Jamie didn't even have the decency to excuse himself to snort his white powder in solitude. Instead, he simply turned around to face the wall, hoping the microphone reflection filter would hide his quick double snort of his bullet before launching into another take. That take wasn't the keeper.

Although the four-hour slot quickly flew by, Casey was adamant about getting the recording down, however long it would take. At the end of the day they had finally pieced together a decent demo, but it still needed considerable editing to make it sound professional. The increasing claustrophobia of being stuck in a small room with amateur rockstars with substance abuse problems who didn't value his work was quickly making his blood boil.

"Ok," Casey said, hiding his frustration. "That's probably good enough to start editing and mixing. Let me get back to you with a rough mix after the weekend."

Casey hadn't thought about collecting payment beforehand. He trusted the band could correctly estimate their proficiency in the studio, so he was now looking at over eight hours of work plus the extra editing and mixing work that lay ahead of him. He realized just how misplaced his trust in the band was. He felt stuck between a slowly dwindling checking account and a low-budget band he already couldn't stand. He wished for either the rock or the hard place.

"How would you like to pay for the session today? We went quite a bit over the four hours we originally scheduled so we might need to factor that in?"

"I thought we agreed on $100 for a finished song?" Jamie snapped back, his pupils dilated to the size of eight-balls.

"Yeah for sure!" Casey blurted out, "But I thought we could finish it in four hours like you said."

"Sorry dude, that's just Donnie. He didn't realize you couldn't fix his drums," Jamie quickly motioned to Donnie who was packing up his drums, oblivious to the conversation, his t-shirt soaked in sweat and radiating body odor.

"Besides, it took us forever to set up so that's on you." Jamie stared at Casey, grinding his teeth and tapping his feet to a non-existent beat.

"Well, it's a part of the recording process to get sounds that you're happy with. The four hours include some setup time to get your tracks sounding good." Casey didn't mention the time it took him to set up the studio so that it was ready for them when they came in. He tried to be as efficient as possible but the fact that these guys had none of the foresight or the friendship to understand what went into preparing the session was slowly pushing him closer to the edge.

"Well, we didn't know that. That's not really what we were coming in here for. We just wanted to play a live song and have a demo at the end of it and that's what we agreed on."

Casey knew that there was no reasoning with Jamie. He was in full frontman mode and wanted to be treated like the rockstar he thought he was.

"Ok, let me get back to you with a finished demo, but would you mind paying the $100 for the session today seeing as the track is almost done?" Casey asked.

"No way man, I'm paying for the finished song only. Send me the mp3 when you're done."

Casey sighed and silently weighed his options. He could keep fighting, but he was unlikely to get his $100 without finishing the project. He'd probably have to put in another eight hours of post-production just to be proud of having his name attached to the project, which would mean that his hourly rate was tanking to well below minimum wage. The other option was to abandon the project entirely and just ghost the band after they left the studio, but he felt oddly attached to the time he already spent and he wanted something to show for it. He mustered up a smile and assured Jamie, "I'll be in touch after the weekend."

Yes, I will finish your shitty record. Yes, I will make it sound good. No, I will never talk to you again.

After hours of painstaking editing work to make their drummer sound even halfway proficient at his job, Casey began mixing the song. Casey enjoyed mixing and often practiced with multitracks he found on the internet. He thought he was a decent enough mixing engineer because when he compared his practice mixes to other songs he heard on the radio, they sounded pretty close to those commercial recordings. He blended the drums together with the rest of the instruments. The kick drum and bass guitar played in sync, not that the actual players were any help with that. The guitars slammed through both sides of the stereo spectrum and the synth leads interweaved with the vocal lines. After adding effects and trying new tricks he read about online, Casey felt happy with his mix. It was a far cry from the initial recording that sounded so raw it would give you food poisoning. It wasn't as spectacular as he wanted it to be, but he refused to spend more time on such a shitty band.

He finished the mix by Sunday night and sent it off to Jamie for feedback. He was hoping they would like what they heard so they would finish the project and pay him what they owed him. He thought about how awful his first session had been—how many mistakes he had made and things he hadn't thought about preparing for. He wondered what he could do better next time. He showed up ready and prepared. He tried to be as professional as possible. What was it that made the entire session so frustrating?

Let's hope they like the mix. He shut off his studio and spent the rest of the night tossing and turning, his studio business already failing before it even got off the ground.

CHAPTER 3
STAIRWAY, DENIED.

One blog post with no traffic, one Instagram feed post with 5 likes, no stories because who cares, another argument with a troll on an audio forum, and it was Wednesday. Casey was overwhelmed with all the advice he found about improving his online presence. He thought he could make some progress on promoting his studio website but it felt like drinking from a fire hydrant. The more he read about what he should do, the more exhausted he became. The more options he found, the less confident he felt about continuing. He hated how much extra stuff he had to do just so that he could find artists to work with.

Casey hadn't heard back from the band so he emailed Jamie again to follow up. No response. Two days of flailing his arms at trying to grow his online presence later, Casey followed up again and immediately got a response back.

"Hey dude, sorry about this. We're not happy with the feel of the track so we're going to go with someone else. Thanks for trying anyway."

Thanks for trying?!? They had a deal, even if the pay was terrible. Casey's chest sank in frustration. Tapping his fingers on the desk, he pondered his options. Garbage's "I'm Only Happy When it Rains" came on his playlist, increasing his agitation.

Casey was pissed off, but he thought better than to blow up so he diplomatically emailed back, "I'm sorry you feel that way. I'd be happy to make any revisions if you'd like to get closer to what you have in mind?" He knew revisions were going to make the project drag on even longer, but he was desperate for a portfolio item.

Jamie messaged back, "It's ok, don't worry about it. We're going to table this song for now."

Casey replied, "All right, I understand. When would be a good time to meet to settle up the payment then?"

Jamie's grammar took a nosedive into middle-school dumbass mode, "im not gonna pay for something were not using dude."

Casey stared at the screen in rage. He started typing, hitting the keys with the animal ferocity of deathmetal snare fills, "You fucking owe me for what we agreed on DUDE! It's not my fault your drummer can't play for shit. I spent three times as much time as you said it would take just to make your shitty song sound like a halfway decent demo! Pay me my money!"

The words sat there and just as he was about to hit send, he stopped. There was no way they were paying him for his work. He suspected Jamie would be the type of guy that would talk shit about him to everyone. Besides, Jamie probably spent his $100 on another bag of blow. Did he really want to start his professional career with a shitty reputation because he exploded on the first band that took advantage of him? It wasn't worth it and there had to be a better way to get started. He deleted his email reply. He looked at the clock in the corner of his computer screen before closing it. It wasn't just five o'clock somewhere. It was 5 o'clock here and he needed a drink.

Dr. Roberts was the type of local dive bar you could find in every town. Cheap drinks, above-average pub food, random sports team allegiances on the walls. What outweighed the annoying times the bar was full because of some random football game were all the other times the bar was mostly empty of hooligans, yet filled with great music blaring out of the speakers.

A providential playlist seemingly curated for Casey's exact mood played overhead: "The Complaint Department" by Lykke Li, "Milionária" by ROSALÍA and "I Will Survive" by Cake. You can complain, wish and settle for surviving. Or you can put in the work and thrive.

Casey drowned his sorrows over a drink with his friend John. John had kept his job as a junior account executive at Oasis Online Ops and before Casey frustration-fucked-off-out-the-door they became good buddies during Casey's time there. Casey needed a break from his setbacks and he didn't want to confront his slowly diminishing savings—$2,497.03 after groceries, gas, and a broken toilet—until the following morning. Casey hated the thought of going back to the marketing agency, but at least it was a steady pay-check. He quit the job for a reason and he doubted his boss would take him back, even if John put in a good word for him. He'd rather take the pain of uncertainty than the suffocation of a terrible job.

"I'm so pissed off at these guys!" Casey exclaimed, his rage bubbling to the surface. John was the under-standing type who never judged you for your actions, however stupid they were. He was cynical yet friendly, and had a matter-of-fact way of looking at the universe.

"Yeah, it sucks man. But there's nothing you can do about it except move on, right?"

"I suppose. I just hate being back at square one. I thought I could at least get started and have something to show for it. I don't even have a shitty recording to put on my portfolio. If the amateur bands don't even want to pay me for my work, how am I ever going to get more established bands to care?"

"I don't know if that's the way to think about it," John said.

"What do you mean?"

"Well, remember those stupid greenhouse guys I had to work with?"

"The stoners?" Casey asked.

"Yeah, exactly. Remember how awful that working relationship was?"

Casey laughed, "Yeah, I vaguely remember you bitching about it back then…"

"They could never get their shit together. They couldn't answer a single question about their business, and then when we tried to help them, we got blamed for everything that went wrong. They weren't happy with anything we did for them. We worked on their branding and it wasn't cool enough. We even gave them detailed plans based on customer research that they never implemented."

"Sounds kind of like my band," Casey admitted. "Whatever happened to that account? I remember showing up one day and they weren't on the calendar anymore?"

"Turns out they weren't paying their bills and we were working for them for free. I think our CEO is still going after them through collections," John chuckled and shook his head. "I think it just goes to show that there will always be shitty customers around that don't appreciate what you do and want everything for nothing."

Casey nodded, "I think you're right."

"But hey, I don't know much about starting your own thing. I like being an employee. I couldn't deal with the uncertainty like you," John shrugged and continued. "However, I know someone who you could talk to. My wife's brother works in the music industry. He's a big-shot musicpreneur, whatever that means. Helps people find success through marketing and promoting themselves. He's quite a bit older than Jen and we still have yet to figure out quite how he makes money. He definitely makes more than me, which made me jealous at first until I realized there was simply no competing with the guy. He's nice. I'll cc you on an email. He might be able to help you out."

Casey was hesitant. "I don't know man. I hate all this marketing and business stuff. I just want to help musicians make music. Why do I have to have to do all this extra stuff if I just want to make music?"

John warned, "I'm not sure it quite works out that way. Remember Field of Dreams?"

"I prefer Wayne's World 2," Casey shot back.

John laughed, "Regardless, even if you build it, you can't be sure they will come. Let me at least make the introduction?"

"Alright, I suppose," Casey nodded.

"I'll warn you though. He's a pretty busy guy and does a lot of high-profile work so make sure you grab any opportunity he gives you to meet."

"Of course, no problem."

Casey's frustration gnawed at his insides. He hated marketing and wanted nothing to do with it. It was a waste of time that was taking away from his real passion of working on music. He shuddered at the sleaziness of selling and wanted to distance himself from everything that reminded him of his previous employer. Toby Keith's "I Love This Bar" came on the overhead stereo and Casey groaned.

"Another drink?" John asked.

CHAPTER 4
A MAN OF ROUTINE

The man rose with the sun like clockwork. He hadn't set an alarm in years. The sun flooded the master bedroom through the giant second-story window of his mansion that looked over the city. A man of habit, his mental triggers caused a succession of events that made up his morning routine. The peeing begat the washing of the hands which begat the daily prescriptions and vitamins. Omeprazole, 40 mg. Loratadine, 10 mg. Zocor. Glucosamine. Vitamin B, D, E and the rest of the alphabet. The swallowing of the pills triggered the brushing of the teeth. One trigger begat another. Begat. Begat. Moving mindfully from one habit to another helped him achieve a mindless morning routine that created the energy needed to get through the day. His triggers created a chain of events that needed no conscious energy, only the muscle memory of knowing which trigger to pull next.

He flowed from the bathroom into his private yoga

studio downstairs. He passed the pictures as he moved down the staircase. Past the pictures of celebrities, framed golden records and shelves of golden gramophones that sometimes had his name. Others were gifts from appreciative students, a form of payback they never let him turn down.

The old man cleared his throat. "Alexa, play my morning routine," he said softly, his feet firm against the yoga mat. The soothing tones of Ólafur Arnalds emanated from the room as he moved through his yoga poses, the caressing atmosphere of "Near Light" aiding his movements. The smooth shifts of endless repetitions were effortless.

Balasana. Marjaryasana. Bhujangasana. The ambient music faded into "saman," the gentle piano setting the mood.

Uttana Shishosana. Ustrasana. Balasana. Bharmanasana. His mind was completely focused. His body, completely regulated.

Dandasana. Ardha Purvottanasana. Halsana. He floated from one pose to another, his limbs seemingly impervious to gravity.

Supta Parivrtta Garudasana. Apanasana. "20:17" bloomed from the speakers.

And finally, Savasana. Eyes closed. Corpse pose.

Through years of repetition he knew exactly the amount of moves he needed to go through until Alexa would move him into the meditation portion of his routine. "Start Meditation," the robot voiced. The sounds of the speakers changed to waves and bird calls. His heart rate slowed and his breath deepened into the calmness of his mind.

Meditation is simple, but not easy. A cacophonous world has evolved our senses. Our attention is attacked with 10,000 ads every day and the hyperactivity of our monkey minds make stillness a struggle. Meditation helped him focus; it helped him *respond* to the world, instead of *reacting* to what the world wanted from him. However, even after all these years, sitting still and focusing on his breath to keep his mind from wandering was simultaneously the easiest and the hardest thing he did. Sitting and enjoying the silence and stillness was an important part of taking the world head on and he was grateful for today's calm inner monologue. He contemplated nothing in particular, just the in and the out of his breath, while he listened to the world around him. The birds outside the window and the hum of his house. The shaman had told him during his last retreat how we are all beings of energy vibrating at certain frequencies. We go through cycles of ups and downs, crests and troughs, simultaneously coexisting with the good and the bad. Our frequencies move through their cycles, higher frequencies moving faster and faster, with life getting faster, harder and more complex until the ups and downs become indistinguishable from one another and you simply learn to be one with what the world throws at you.

The waves faded away and the man came back to center. "It is time for your morning smoothie," the robot chimed.

In the kitchen, the man prepared his daily smoothie, a ritual that was just as important as the rest of his morning routine. It had been his breakfast for decades.

Some entrepreneurs conserve decision making energy by always wearing the same outfits. He was a little more vain than that, although the mindset made sense. His smoothie was his variation on the theme. Wearing the same thing every day meant one less thing to decide, leaving brainpower for more creative work. When he found clothes that made him comfortable and confident, he bought every color that suited his olive skin. Instead of wearing the same thing every day, he color-coordinated outfits hanging in his wardrobe so he never had to spend time figuring out what to wear. His habits encouraged less trivial decision-making so he could focus his creative juices on things that mattered.

He preserved his mental energy by never making a single decision until he was ready to face the world. The smoothie was a staple of that routine. A healthy mélange of fruits, vegetables, seeds and protein. One part spinach, two parts fruit, a spoonful of whatever seeds he was into that month, yogurt and the occasional crushed up psilocybin et voilà! That was breakfast.

The man took a few sips of the smoothie and set the glass back on the granite countertop of the kitchen island overlooking his living room. The morning sun hit the water at just the right angle to make his pool glimmer.

His friend, a TV show puppet-pastor from Pittsburgh, had shown him the health benefits of swimming as an alternative to running. "Not as hard on your knees and you'll get the same workout," he told him a lifetime ago. Shortly thereafter he bought the house with the pool overlooking the city. An oasis and a fortress against the rat-race he escaped long ago.

50 laps later and his exercise routine was done. Exercise created energy and mental clarity. His regimen was strict in order to keep his mental game on point. Otherwise he would lose his edge and be at a disadvantage to help his students. He didn't need hours in the gym to feel healthy. An elevated heart rate was all he needed to give him the clarity to face the day. It wasn't until he had taken care of himself that he allowed other people's expectations into his atmosphere. He learned a long time ago that if the first thing he did in the morning was reacting to other people's agendas, he would never find the time to care for himself.

Back in the kitchen, a towel wrapped around his waist and dew drops of pool water and sweat on his face, he made himself a Vietnamese coffee. The coarsely ground, Robusta variety dripped through the special Ca Phe Phin filter a Vietnamese pop star had given him. The coffee brewed while he whisked an egg yolk with condensed milk, creating a fluffy mixture. The Vietnamese filter dripped the strong liquid into a glass. He topped off the liquid with the egg mixture, a delicacy he allowed himself too frequently. The taste instantly conjured up images of the crazy streets of

Hanoi, the tuk tuks and the pedicabs zipping through the city while he played an intensely realistic game of Frogger to get from one side of the street to the other. Vietnam was a perfect example of balance. The craziness of Hanoi's alleys countered with the expansive serenity of Halong Bay.

Smiling. Calm and relaxed. Making time for the simplest of things prepared him to tackle the difficult tasks thrown at him throughout the day. His body ached in the defensive way a body acted after a workout, as a preventative measure against unnecessary aging. He flipped open his laptop on the counter and started one of his instrumental playlists filled with ambient textures, deeply reverb'd percussion and melodic motifs. It was his way of cuing the brain into another routine. 1,000 words later, his minimum writing quota achieved before allowing himself into the real world, he checked his email.

Every day, countless emails would pour in from his students who shared wins with him that he had helped them achieve. He counted their wins with them and celebrated their success, grateful for the opportunity to help them make an impact. Only after focusing on himself, his own creativity, and his students, did he flick the switch to turn on the outside world.

SUCCESS STRATEGY #1
MAKE SUCCESS A HABIT

Make your routine a non-negotiable habit in your life, even if you don't feel like it. It's the people who show up, especially when they don't feel like it, that succeed. The easiest thing in the world is to give into procrastination. When you procrastinate you might start comparing yourself to somebody more successful than you and think that you will never be as successful as them. You can achieve anything you want as long as you continuously show up to work on moving yourself closer to your goal. Making your tasks a habit is the key to creating continuous improvement. A little bit of work every day, no matter how small, will sooner or later add up to a significant accomplishment.

You are what you repeatedly do. Noah writes but your creativity might manifest itself differently. Put the time in and don't make it negotiable. You'll fail all the time but unless you completely give up, you'll never truly fail. Think about the goal you want to achieve next year and ask yourself:

"What is the one thing that if I were to do repeatedly, would move me closer to that goal?"

Get the worksheets at
www.YouGetWhatYouGiveBook.com

CHAPTER 5

WHAT GOT YOU HERE WON'T GET YOU THERE

Casey groaned awake. He rolled over to check his phone: 9:14 AM. His head throbbed from too many drinks with John. He stumbled into the bathroom, splashed his face awake with cold water and lazily brushed his teeth, toothpaste dripping down his chin. He struggled into his studio and hit the power conditioner with his toe, turning on the workstation. He made strong, black coffee and then sat down to check his emails. Sure enough, at the top of his inbox was an email from John.

To: Casey

CC: Noah

Subject: Intro?

Hey guys,

Casey, meet Noah. Noah, meet Casey. I think you guys should know each other. Casey is starting a business recording bands and I thought you could help him out with some advice on navigating the business side of the music industry?

I'll leave you guys to it!

Best,
John

As soon as Casey finished reading the intro, Noah's reply came through.

From: Noah

To: Casey

Nice to meet you, Casey. Any friend of John's is a friend of mine. I'd love to hear about your music career and see if I can offer any insights. I'm free for lunch today if you'd like to meet and chat. How is Bridgewater Brewing Co. at noon?

Just the mention of spending an hour talking about marketing made Casey sick to his stomach. Was it the idea of marketing? Or was it the unnecessary "one more beer?" at the end of the night?

Casey remained hesitant. He wasn't interested in selling out. He imagined how this lunch would go, this old dude lecturing him on the same random shit he'd heard in the hallways of Oasis Online Ops. KPIs! Calls to Action! What's the lifetime value of the client?!? The memories reverberated off the walls of Casey's mind, grating high-frequency echoes that fluttered around in his brain, making his hangover worse. But the feeling gnawed at him. What did he have to lose?

His current strategy consisted of shooting darts at an imaginary dartboard that didn't even have any points to help him know how well he was doing. Casey remembered John's warning, "...*make sure you grab any opportunity he gives you to meet.*"

Since Casey had nothing planned for the foreseeable future except hunting for new clients, a task in which he was exceptionally awful at, he agreed to the lunch plans with the mysterious musicpreneur. The worst thing that could happen was a lost lunch hour and some boring chit-chat. He hoped for anything better than that, but as far as worst-case scenarios went, he was fine with it. Casey shrugged off his hangover and got ready for lunch.

Bridgewater Brewing Co. had the best beer and burgers in town, and it was exactly what Casey needed to fill his stomach and extinguish his leftover headache. He pulled open the heavy metal doors and the unmistakable smell of yeast, hops, and malt wafted through the air. David Bowie's "Fashion" riffed with funk and soul overhead. He peered around the restaurant looking for Noah. The only likely candidate was the older man chatting with the waitstaff by the bar. He had an aura around him that Casey couldn't put his finger on. He dressed business casual like the many executives he had mingled with before, but his clothes seemed more stylish. His shirt fit him better than any of the oversized dress shirts he'd seen Corporate wearing. He looked oddly confident and in his environment. Noah looked over to him, smiled and waved. He made the waitstaff laugh one more time before walking over to greet him.

He met Noah at the bar and they exchanged pleasantries while they decided on their orders. Once their orders were in, Noah asked Casey for the details on his new business venture. While elaborating on the nightmare of his first week as a studio owner Noah listened intently. Noah had an intense attention about him and Casey felt silly describing the escapades of the previous weekend. As Casey finished, Noah smiled and sat back in his chair. The restaurant felt eerily silent, as if the music had stopped on cue, but then he noticed the outro to "Cold Desert" by Kings of Leon slowly fading back onto the loudspeakers.

"You're not trying to make an impact," Noah stated.

"What does that mean?" Casey was taken aback by Noah's abrupt answer. He frowned, feeling like Noah had sized him up and judged him instantly.

Noah shrugged it off, "You're never going to make an impact if you're always going after lackluster bands that don't appreciate the work you're doing for them." Noah shook his head as if shrugging off any band in the universe that fit this mental picture.

He continued, "You don't want to position your services as being for bands that aren't serious about making an impact with their music."

"I thought that band was serious! It wasn't my fault I didn't realize how hard it would be to record them. They told me they could do it in four hours, but I probably spent closer to twenty hours on the whole project," Casey said, remembering the excruciating time he spent editing the drummer's terrible tom fills.

"Whether or not you think it's your fault is irrelevant. It's still your responsibility. Your first mistake was trying to think in hours when estimating a project, and then your second mistake was allowing them to blow past the agreed upon time without renegotiating."

"I didn't feel comfortable stopping the project midway through just to talk money," Casey sighed.

"That's understandable, and actually a great reason why having an hourly rate isn't good for anybody." Noah told Casey how having an hourly rate puts the project in the back seat. "When you sell hours, you make the band hurry up because they want to finish things as fast as possible. A rushed job isn't what you're after. You're looking for quality work to build your portfolio. A band that's trying to do everything as cheap as possible doesn't see the value in your additional work, such as editing and tuning, because they assume you're going to take care of it." He ended his monologue saying, "If their drums are not in time and their vocals are out of tune, it's not their fault."

Casey didn't like being patronized and was starting to feel annoyed at the old man, "Of course it's their fault!" he exclaimed. "They should know how to play their instruments."

Noah shrugged, "Sure, but you're ultimately to blame because it's your project and you should treat it like you're the leader. They don't know how to make a record. They just know how to play songs."

"Yeah, they definitely didn't care about all the extra work. They didn't even pay me at all," Casey said and sighed.

Casey told Noah about Jamie's rejection and how they hadn't liked the feel of the song. He admitted to almost rage-replying back to him because he was so pissed off at the end of the project.

"They came to you for a result and you didn't deliver the transformation they were looking for. How much did you like your new business venture at that point?" Noah asked with a chuckle.

"I hated it even more than the job I already quit!" Casey exclaimed and took a sip of his beer.

"It all goes back to who you want to work with and what kind of impact you want to make with your work," Noah said while Casey nodded along. Casey felt like he had wasted hours reading articles that were all spewing simple business tactics while the real win was in developing a strategy to make good art.

Noah didn't seem to believe in charging hourly at all, although he had some caveats.

He said, "Let's take your hourly rate for instance. For a lot of freelancers, an hourly rate makes total sense. A programmer clocks in and out and as long as they're diligent and productive, they can charge a healthy hourly rate because of the deliverables that are tied to their work. And for certain jobs in the industry, an hourly rate may be the only way you can charge for your work. But for something more creative, an hourly rate encourages sloppiness, especially with a novice band. It's probably why the band disliked your work."

"I made it sound as good as I could," Casey sighed.

"And you probably did an excellent job. But they may not even realize why they disliked your work. They might feel like their sloppy performance was because you made them rush through their hours. At that point, the easiest person to blame is you."

Casey nodded into his beer, taking in all of his newbie mistakes.

Noah continued, "The question isn't about how *quickly* you can get things done. It's how *good* you can make their music sound. Of course, you may want to do that in the least amount of time possible, but that comes with experience. The big question you should be asking yourself isn't how much you should be charging per hour, it's how much you can help them make an impact."

He laid out his right hand, palm facing up and said, "Are you trying to help make music that you're proud of?" he asked, while opening his left palm, "or are you just wanting to fill up your day with billable hours like an attorney trying to fleece their corporate client for as much as they can?"

"I want to help make music that I enjoy," Casey responded, instinctually pointing to Noah's right hand.

"That's what I thought. But if all you're doing is rushing through hours, then you both end up with a bad product. It won't help them in their career and it also won't get you extra gigs because all you have on your portfolio is sloppy work. And they certainly won't refer anybody to you if you're known for sloppy work, even if it is technically *their* fault. It's a lose-lose situation that brings zero meaningful impact to anyone. A record is a piece of art and it deserves the time necessary to work on it to make it the best it can be. It's a race to the bottom if you're constantly fishing for low-value clients that only want the cheapest option. You may think that you need to lower your rate in order to compete, but it actually has the opposite effect," Noah said with a tone of experience.

"I thought the cheaper the product, the easier it is for more people to buy?" Casey said.

Noah waved this statement away in an instant.

"Do you think music is a commodity, like a barrel of grain?" Noah asked.

"Well no...but,"

Noah cut him off, "It might be true on a simplistic supply and demand graph in an Intro to Econ class, and it may work when you're selling certain products, but it's a myth when it comes to finding clients. The lower your rate, the worse your clients are."

Casey remained skeptical, but Noah was adamant about his point.

"Think of it this way: if *you* don't even see yourself as being worth a decent rate, *why would somebody else?* Do you want to compete with some Buttrock Barry down the street that'll do a recording session for $5/hour?"

Casey shook his head and laughed.

"Then don't. Simply stop comparing yourself to that. Offer something that's more valuable. Position yourself not as 'more expensive' but as a 'better investment in their music.' If you give them a price per hour, they'll rush through the studio time so they can pay less."

Casey thought about the frustration he felt when the band kept looking at the clock and compromised on the quality of their performance because of it.

"How do I make them think that I'm more valuable than Buttrock Barry down the street?" Casey asked.

"Are you familiar with Obi-Wan Kenobi?" Noah asked with a smirk.

"The Jedi?" Casey stammered.

"Yes. Think of yourself as Obi-Wan Kenobi and the musician you're working with as Luke."

Casey hesitated, trying to follow Noah's logic.

"Let's just imagine your next client's name is Luke. So, Luke has a song, and he's a great musician, but he has no idea what he needs to do to make that song sound like the songs he loves on the radio. He spent all his life perfecting his instrument chops, his singing, and his songwriting. He knows how to play, but he has no idea about the power of engineering, the force if you will…" Casey laughed at Noah's absurd analogy, but he continued on.

"So, he's lost. He wants something. He's seeking guidance, and *look, Obi-Wan Kenobi, you're his only hope!*" Noah emphasized his final sentence with air quotes and they both burst into laughter.

"And then he meets you. You took a different path than he did. You learned the ways of The Audio and you have production chops in a technical sense, whereas he has a musical sense that needs translated to that final product you know how to create with him."

Noah kept the one-way conversation going, "Transformation can't be measured in hours, and neither can value. So, when you're offering transformation and impact, you're dismissing the people who only see hours. When you pay for five bucks an hour, you get what you pay for. When you pay for transformation, you get results. But comparing the two is like comparing apples and a zebra. You have to frame it as a transformation, not a burden, because every time they're in the studio, the clock is ticking. You want to price yourself on impact, not on hours. That's why flat rates and packages work so much better. If you create packages, you take the worry of time out of the equation and the band can relax knowing that an extra hour here and there isn't going to cost them extra."

"But what if they take forever to get a good take?" Casey asked.

"You should keep that in mind and manage expectations from the start. You should make it abundantly clear that everyone should know their parts prior to coming to the studio and you reserve the right to cut the sessions if they are simply using your time as practice time for them. That's not only unprofessional of them, but also insulting to your time. Managing expectations in that way will help you control the situation so that you're not taken advantage of."

The server arrived with their order and as soon as she sat down their plates, Casey's face sank. Casey had ordered a Black 'n' Blue Burger with blue cheese, red onions, spicy chilies, and Bridgewater's signature Baja sauce. Noah ordered the vegetarian option, a black bean patty with avocado, onion straws, and spicy honey mustard. "Land of Confusion" by Genesis came on the overhead speakers and Casey told the server politely that his order was wrong. Instead of the Black 'n' Blue Burger he had looked forward to, he was stuck with a standard cheeseburger.

The server profusely apologized, "I'm so sorry, I must've gotten it mixed up completely."

"It's ok…it's totally fine. I can eat this, but would you be able to bring me a side of the Baja sauce to go with it?"

"Of course!" the server said and swooped back into the kitchen.

Mere moments later, much to Casey's surprise, the

server returned from the kitchen, not only with his side of sauce, but his original order as well.

"They're running around like chickens with their heads cut off in there!" the server laughed, "Here's your order, sorry for the mix-up!" The server eyed Noah and grinned. Noah mouthed a thank you as she left.

Noah smirked and gave Casey a "it happens" sort of shrug and dug into his burger.

Casey had looked up Noah before lunch and was astounded by the musical celebrities he had been associated with in the past. He really wanted to ask him personal questions but he had a feeling that for someone so eager to share his thoughts, he was still a very private man.

"Impact," Casey muttered in between bites.

"That's right," Noah said. "You're not in the business of selling your time, you're in the business of creating an impact for your client in the music industry."

Noah continued, "It's much easier to get clients when you're looking for a win-win situation. Can I tell you a story of what I learned from one of my first mentors?" Noah asked, grabbing a fry and dipping it in ketchup.

"By all means!" Casey nodded enthusiastically.

"One of my first jobs was as a dishwasher at a restaurant. It was a popular restaurant and had a well-known chef manning the wheel of the ship. And I was just a kid lucky enough to have a job so I could spend my take-home pay on records. CDs, vinyl, bootleg tapes, remember those musical artifacts of history?" Noah chuckled.

"Dreams" By Fleetwood Mac played softly in the background, quieter than the loud, remastered and hyper compressed songs that accompanied it on the restaurant's playlist.

"Anyways, imagine Ratatouille except I didn't have an imaginary talking rat as my mentor. Instead, I had this chef who had some success in the industry before he changed careers and opened up a restaurant. He told me one of the most valuable lessons I have kept with me ever since." Noah finally took a bite out of his burger to savor the suspense as Casey waited for the big reveal.

"The only currency that's worth more than its weight in gold is a hit song. There is no substitute for a great song. No amount of marketing, expensive equipment, or glossy album covers will substitute for a great song. It's the only thing that matters. You're only as good as the songs you've worked on, so you better choose your songs wisely if you want to command respect in the industry. A recorded song is a business card. You want to help bands have the nicest business card because if they get recognition for their music, that recognition washes onto you. If you choose your projects wisely and do everything in your power to help those artists make an impact, fortune will flow your way."

"But that doesn't really help me figure out what to charge for my services. What about people who just

call and ask how *much to record a song?*" Casey interjected.

Noah was unfazed. "You're not getting it. If you're
trying to deliver impact in their career it's not about
how fast you can get things done, it's about how well
the final product feels. You can certainly start with
an hourly rate based on whatever you're comfortable
with, but under no circumstances should you cut corners in the quality of your work. If they don't see your
work as an investment in their music career, then they
simply aren't the right client for you. Running after
bands that don't see the value you bring and just want
the cheapest product available is a losing race to the
bottom. You are an investment in their career and they
should see that. However, it's up to you to persuade
them to see it your way. What is the valuable impact
you have on their music?"

Noah paused and let his words hang in the air.
Casey didn't realize he was asking a question because
so far Noah had been peppering him with strong statements.

"What is my impact?" Casey asked.

"Yes, why should they hire you? How does hiring
you help them make an impact in their career? People
are always looking for *what's in it for them.* It's naive
to think that they're coming to you because you're so
awesome. They're coming to you because they want
something you might deliver. What is that? What is
the value you bring to the table? Businesses exist to

solve problems, and make no mistake, you are running a business, not a hobby."

Casey nodded, realizing the enormity of his undertaking. He was treating his studio like a hobby, just like he did when he had an actual income. Running a business was an entirely different beast.

"So what problem are you trying to solve for your customers?" Noah asked.

Casey stammered because he'd never thought about putting it into the client's perspective. "Well...I help them sound more professional. Their songs will sound more like the records they like so much, or that they hear on the radio."

Noah nodded, "What else?"

Casey continued, "Their songs will sound more like a commercial release opposed to a bedroom demo, which they would end up with if they worked on it themselves."

"So, you're saving them time *and* helping them succeed?" Noah asked.

"Well, I've never put it that way but I suppose."

"And what problem are you solving for them?"

"I guess their problem is that they don't know how to record professionally, and anything they try themselves sounds awful and amateurish. They don't have the equipment they need and they only have a basic understanding of what audio engineering even means."

"Ok, now we're getting somewhere. Do you see how

you have to position yourself so that they understand the value that you bring?"

Casey nodded while taking a big bite of his hamburger. Casey was beginning to get it, but it just made him realize how much he still had to learn. He took the last sip of his beer while trying to put everything Noah said into perspective. He came here expecting a boring conversation about the same sort of marketing jargon he was only too happy to escape, but instead he felt grateful for Noah's insights. Noah eyed him and grinned.

"It's a lot to take in, isn't it," Noah stated.

"That's one way to put it."

"Tell you what. If you'd like to keep chatting about this stuff, I'd be happy to have lunch with you every week until you've got a game plan. You can keep me abreast of what's going on and I'll give you any advice I think will be useful. How's that?"

Casey was hesitant. How much was that going to cost? His savings were already dwindling and he had no leads on new clients. He must've been wearing his worries on his face because Noah read his mind and said, "There's no charge. Just cover the lunches and we'll see where it takes us."

Without hesitation, Casey said, "Deal."

As Casey settled up their bill, Noah said, "There's a lot more to learn about finding your worth and making an impact. I'm excited to see what you come up with."

They shook hands and Casey left Bridgewater Brewing, his hopeless anxiety replaced with confident optimism.

SUCCESS STRATEGY #2
PRIORITIZE IMPACT

Decide what high-quality work is for you and what standards are non-negotiable when it comes to delivering value as a creative. You only have so much time on this earth and you are 100% responsible for what you do with that time.

Do you want to chase down frustrations in the form of people who don't value you, or do you want to find people who share your vision for making a difference with their work?

Success takes time and you'll take a few years for people to see you as an overnight success. Make sure that you use that time wisely to create value that adds impact to your life and those who you want to serve.

Prioritize the people who show up. The people who raise their hands and believe that you can help are the ones you should focus on. The people who tear you down, criticize you on the internet or don't care what you have to say don't need your attention. Flip the power around and make your H8ERS your MOTIV8ERS instead. The trolls will always come out of the woodwork to criticize you. Just blow them a kiss and go on your way. They'll go back under their bridge, and you'll cross onto your next adventure.

If you believe in the importance of your work and you keep doing it in a methodical way, sooner or later some of those people will notice. Help one person make an impact in their lives. That impact will positively affect them and those around them. Do that enough times and your impact will be snowballed because of the network effect you'll have created with your intentions.

Get the worksheets to create your success plan at www.YouGetWhatYouGiveBook.com

CHAPTER 6
CREATIVITY IN THE KITCHEN

I f the man's body was a temple, his kitchen was his workshop. Noah slid his custom Don Nguyen knife from the sleeve and gave it a quick sharpen on the steel. He flipped it around in his hands, admiring the craftsmanship. He was lucky enough to acquire one of the knives before they commanded four figures and sold out instantly. When you're too good to ignore, you're in demand and you command a premium. Although he always appreciated a good deal, he thought fondly of how exclusive the knives had gotten so far. Noah thought of it like an undervalued stock or an early-stage angel investment you could sell for many multiples its initial price. Of course, this knife was never going back on the market. It was a collector's item, although he still used it as a workhorse, never understanding why people bought things only to put them away, never to be used.

"Backburner" by Alan Garr played softly in the

kitchen and Noah wondered how much of his advice had landed with the kid at lunch. Whenever he met with a potential student, he always gauged them on a few criteria.

The first was the amount of drive he could see in their eyes. If they looked like a race horse eager to hurtle through twelve furlongs, he assumed they were ready for the marathon they needed to start training for.

If they asked questions, shared freely and looked like they were listening he assumed they were open to learning and improvement.

The last criteria he would know soon enough. It was only through action that one could thrive and depending on the amount of action the kid would take in the following week, he could almost predict his success, like a graph where the X-axis was Action and the Y-axis was Success. An object at rest stays at rest and he knew the kid needed initial momentum to be off to the races.

The kid had passed the first test when he received the wrong hamburger. He could always gauge a person by how well they treated their servers, and Noah had asked them to deliberately mix up Casey's order to see how the kid would react. He had been graceful and accepting of the mistake so Noah knew he was a good human at heart.

He remembered many times where his potential students had gone off at the server, taking their frustration out on them instead of accepting the mistake for what it was: a simple miscommunication that didn't need name-calling or elevated annoyance. Those students had been abandoned to their own devices without a follow-up meeting. Although you had multiple opportunities to make an impact, you only had one chance to make a first impression.

His workspace was laid out in front of him on the kitchen island: A plastic cutting board for meats, a wooden one for everything else. An assortment of salts, herbs and spices. Knives for every necessity, accessories for every action. He found cooking to be creative, yet it was a welcome break from career creativity because every meal had a definite beginning, middle and end. He had spent years chasing continuous career creativity, growing his name in the music industry to rise to elite status. But career creativity was endless. There was always another goal to hit, another milestone to reach, another to-do on the list. High-achievers fail to recognize burnout because they're too busy feeding their workaholism and moving the goalposts to an undefined level of success, never stopping to savor the success they already achieved. He had taught himself to cook as a reprieve from the race.

He approached cooking with the mindset of a student, that of the consummate beginner practicing the fundamentals. Cooking was the intersection of science and art, a creative pursuit not unlike music production, which combined the art of songwriting with the science of audio engineering.

Music is about balance in the same way that adjusting the taste of a dish balances out its flavor. When

Noah cooked, he always asked himself how he could make a dish better until the harmony of flavors was perfect to his taste buds. A bit of salt to add depth. A squeeze of lemon to make it brighter. Cooking required some essential skills that, when mastered, you could improvise, like an accomplished saxophone player masterfully weaving his notes around "Giant Steps." Although to be fair, the bright side of cooking compared to jazz was that you didn't need to know everything about it to be a great chef—the fundamentals were enough so that you knew when to break the rules.

The four building blocks of cooking were simple, but they weren't easy to master. Every recipe had four elements: salt, fat, acid, and heat. Salting was the chemical reaction that transformed the food. If salt brought out the flavor, the acid made it bloom. From lemon juice to cheese, the way Noah used acid opened up the richness of the food. Then, depending on what dish he was making, the interplay between the type of heat he used and the type of fat—Olive Oil in the Mediterranean, butter in Scandinavia, Ghee in India—was crucial to how the food cooked. He was told long ago by his mentors: If you master these four building blocks, you'll become a better cook by instinct instead of relying on paint-by-numbers recipes. Noah had mastered the simple, four-part equation and he now only needed his taste buds to tell him what the food needed.

He rolled the pink Himalayan salt around with his fingers. Such an important stitch in the fabric of our history. To the untrained, salt is simply lumped in with the rest of the spices but it played a much more important role. It's a chemical so essential to society it could grow economies, inspire religious ceremonies and topple empires. The word salary itself was derived from the Latin word salt, and whether or not Roman workers were paid in the chemical was irrelevant. Regardless, Noah enjoyed the underlying meaning of salt being a unit of wealth much more so than the made-up dollar figures of faith in his stock portfolio. The value of salt was intrinsic to itself. It could transform any food from basic and boring to flavorful and bold. Although he liked the Himalayan salt, the baseless claims that it was healthier than normal sea salt bothered him. He knew the high cost of the pink rock was mostly due to marketing, the never-ending pursuit of advertising agencies creating placebo effects through their ads to deceive the public for profit. The Himalayan moniker was a misnomer in itself since most of the impure rock was harvested in the Salt Range mountains of Pakistan. But of course, no Chief Marketing Officer would pull off a marketing campaign touting the health benefits of Pakistani Salt in a post 9/11 America. It was a shame because his travels through Pakistan, India and Sri Lanka had left him with fond memories of incredible food, friendly people and otherworldly, ethereal music full of tonal drums and complex stringed instruments. Traveling changes a person because the memories of those places become a part of them. He incorporated his feelings of travel into his sense of self because the things he learned through understanding other cultures made him a better person. At our core, in every country, we are all the same, getting by with what we have and trying to achieve our dreams.

Music gave him the opportunity to travel the world, and he took advantage of the opportunity to learn about cultures, languages and most importantly: food. As a young man he hated sushi. Cold, raw fish wrapped in seaweed and rice. Dipped into a black sauce with spicy green paste. Gross, he chuckled at the memory. But after helping a few bands go big in Japan, he learned to appreciate the delicacy of a simple tuna on sticky rice with a touch of Wasabi. He learned about "acquired taste" and how simplicity in food brought out the best in its flavors. You don't always have to complicate things. An overstuffed roll that only hides the flavor isn't the best way to savor the sushi. He favored the simpler Nigiri above the overstuffed sushi rolls.

He learned to use all of his senses when he cooked. His mentor told him that we eat with our eyes first so any dish has to look good on the plate. We use our sense of touch to feel the food when we're preparing it. Then we use our sense of smell and taste to decide whether the food is flavorful enough, and our sense of sight and sound to gauge the crackling of the oil on the pan, to know whether the bread is just the right shade of gold, or whether the steak has just the right sear. But your senses are useless if you don't use common sense to tell whether anything you're doing is right. Common sense comes from practice. From repetition. From experience gained. A novice chef who doesn't know the first thing about cooking has all of the five senses everyone else has, except they lack the crucial common sense needed to make a good meal.

CHAPTER 7
TAKING CARE OF BUSINESS

C asey spent the week in a constant state of adding to his never-ending to-do list. The more he thought about what he needed to launch his studio business, the more items he scribbled down. He held his notebook in his hands, realizing that if his to-do list was an old timey scroll it would fall to the floor, roll down the street and over the horizon.

1. Create list of bands to email (again)
2. Listen to their music
3. Decide which ones to reach out to
4. Tweak website
5. Research how to write a bio
6. Rewrite bio
7. Take pictures of the studio for the website (do I need a professional photographer?)
8. Update audio software (and hope my computer doesn't crash)

9. Create a blog? (does a blog make sense?)
10. Make videos? (about what?)
11. Does it make sense to create a podcast? (Who am I to start a podcast anyway?)
12. Open business bank account (do I need an accountant?)
13. Decide on a business entity (LLC? Sole proprietorship? S-Corp?!? *shrug*)
14. Create social media channels. What should I post?
15. Should I offer all kinds of production? Or should I specialize?
16. What should my website offer other than my typical service?

The list went on from there...

He still had no idea how to price himself but he understood that if he was serious about working on great music, he needed to surround himself with musicians that were serious about their art. A great song that sounds professional is a band's most valuable product. It's a business card of sorts, Noah had said. It made sense to him. He wanted his portfolio to work the same way, but he'd never get serious bands if his portfolio was a joke. He looked at his empty website. How could he transform it into the business card *he* needed?

The headline stared at him: *Available for Music Production*. What a vague headline. It didn't say anything about how he would help his potential client make an impact. It didn't answer their questions. What was in it for them? Why would they care to contact him? Let alone hire him for a job. He quickly deleted the headline and wrote, *Tired of the sound of your rehearsal demos? Let's create professional productions you can be proud of.* He was no professional copywriter, but his new headline conveyed more value. At the very least, it gave the potential customer a reason to reach out to him.

That week, one of the many bands he had coldemailed the week before finally got in touch with him. Success! He pumped his fists in the air, aware of his ridiculous excitement.

The band told him they had checked out his website and were curious about what he could do to help them. They had recorded their own song in their rehearsal space and needed someone to mix it to sound more professional. They had a budget of $100 and Casey's excitement dwindled. Was he doomed to be stuck in $100-land forever?

Although it wasn't a huge job, Casey took whatever came his way and asked them to send the recordings over. This time he asked for a 50% deposit before proceeding. He wasn't going to spend any time if they weren't willing to at least put some skin in the game. He figured the mix wouldn't take too long and he hoped that he could create something he could showcase on his website.

The tracks were a disaster, although this time the drummer was in the pocket. He worked on the mix for hours and the end result was *just ok*. Nothing spectacular but nothing terrible either. Casey felt like the job was taking way too long for such a small budget.

He could feel the inner entrepreneur saying, "Dude…you're making less than minimum wage at this point. You've put in much more time than the budget allowed. You need to finish this mix quickly if you're going to stay in the black. Time is money, buddy. You're never getting it back."

However, his inner artist was pleading with him, "But…but…but…this is a piece of art you're involved with that's going to live forever! You can't just ignore it!"

He remembered Noah's message from the weekend before: You have to make sure you contribute the highest quality work you can. Prioritize impact.

Casey thought, *who cares if you put in two extra hours in the long run? It's not a waste of time if you end up with something you're proud of! It's a lose-lose situation for both you and the band if you don't make this sound good! Do work you're proud of now and you'll be proud of it forever.*

Although the tracks had problems, the song was good and the performances were solid, so he decided to listen to his inner artist and spend the time necessary to create something he was proud of. In the end, Casey did his absolute best and made the mix sound leagues beyond what he had started with. He knew he wasn't going to work for peanuts forever, but he needed to showcase his strong work quality before anyone would care to work with him.

Mixing was very much about balance. Casey spent

additional time getting the levels right so that everything was sitting nicely in the song. He added EQ and compression to the drums to make them sound punchy and tight. The drums were the foundation of a good song and this one was energetic and exciting. He knew that if he got the foundation tight and thick, the rest of the song would fall into place. The bass grooved with the kick drum and the guitars sounded edgy without getting in the way of the vocals. The vocals took a while to get right, but after trying out various spaces, reverbs, delays, and parallel processing, he was almost there. He listened to the mix on different monitors, asking himself what would make the mix better. Where was it dull or flat? Did it need to be brighter? After balancing all the aspects of the mix, including the inevitable ego management of a five-piece band wanting five different instruments turned up the loudest, he finally got a mix he was happy with. He felt that he had adequately respected each person's contribution to the song so that the record sounded bigger than the sum of its parts.

Even though it was a struggle, he was genuinely proud of the work he did and he hoped the mix would make an impact for the band.

The following day Casey received an email from the band and they were absolutely *floored* by his work. They never thought someone could take their garage recordings to such a high-quality level and they were so excited about the song that they decided to release it immediately. They proudly gave Casey credit for his work and he finally had an item in his portfolio.

YOU GET WHAT YOU GIVE

Casey's mindset was changing for the better and he was starting to have something to show for it.

CHAPTER 8
WHAT'S THEIR PROBLEM?!

The next week's lunch couldn't come soon enough. Casey was anxious to learn more from Noah about running a business. He was tired of being stuck with $100 clients and he hoped Noah could shed some light on how and what to charge for his services.

This time they met at Kaizen, one of the best Japanese restaurants in town, that always seemed to be pushing the envelope. "Erase/Rewind" by The Cardigans filled the air that wasn't already occupied by the wafting smell of soy sauce, fried batter, miso broth and rice. Kaizen's buffet was affordable and Casey filled his plate with sushi rolls, vegetable tempura, and Yakitori skewers. Noah ordered the Miso soup and an Okonomiyaki pancake, along with a couple of Nigiri rolls.

"So, what's on your mind?" Noah asked, slurping down his Miso soup.

"I've been thinking a lot about what you said about

impact. I need to avoid bands that don't value what I bring to the table, I totally get that. I honestly have no interest in doing another nightmare session like that first one I told you about. But I also don't know how to find those bands, or get them to work with me, other than frantically emailing everybody's band and their grandmother."

"And what else?"

"Well, it seems like such a catch-22. I want to do quality work, but how am I supposed to sell bands on my quality if I only have one track in my portfolio?"

"Quite the chicken or the egg problem isn't it? How do you get clients to believe you're legit if you don't have legit clients in your portfolio?" Noah asked.

"Exactly!"

"This is a common problem for creatives, especially those that need other people to help them create. If you're a painter or a writer, you're self-sufficient. You don't need someone to write or paint with you. You have inspiration, or that's what wannabes like to call it. I learned a long time ago from my buddy Steven that inspiration is a myth. The real name for continuous inspiration in the face of resistance is simply having a work ethic."

Casey nodded in agreement at this distinction.

Noah pressed on, "But if your role makes up a larger creative work, it's hard to showcase your value on your own. If you're a recording engineer, you need an artist to showcase how great your recording skills are, correct?"

"Correct," Casey agreed.

"Sounds like you actually have an overlooked opportunity then," Noah said.

"What do you mean?"

"The artist can't get a great recording without you. They still have a role that needs to be filled. Sometimes that role is filled by someone in the band who's nerdy enough to learn about all the technical stuff the other members can't be bothered with."

"Sure, there's always a guy who speaks audio in the group, usually," Casey said, emphasizing the word audio with air quotes.

"But they're not specialized so they still need an engineer, so I would argue that a band might need you without knowing it, but you still have to prove your value."

"And how do I prove my value if they won't hire me?"

"Simple. Give it away for free," Noah stated without hesitation.

Casey suddenly had some serious doubts about Noah's experience as an entrepreneur. Once again, it seemed like Noah anticipated Casey's misgivings because he chuckled and said, "Now, don't write me off completely. There's a method to the madness."

"Alright, I'd love to hear it because my bank account is running lower by the lunch! Any business advice I've ever heard has usually focused around making money."

Noah laughed, "And you will! Starting out is always

the hardest part, but you should still lead with the desire to make an impact with your work. The best way to do that is doing some free work to get a couple of songs in your portfolio."

Casey mulled this over and found it hard to justify spending so much time without any pay when his expenses were still coming in.

"However, you should always get *something* in return for your free work, and you should also have some restrictions on what you offer as 'free'. They can't take your offer of free work as an opportunity to take advantage of you."

"What do you mean by restrictions?"

"You treat every free session as if you were giving them a courtesy discount, but you still structure your sessions with certain expectations from yourself AND the artist."

"What kind of expectations?"

"If you were working for your ideal rate, what would that include? How much time do they get from you? How many revisions are included? What do you expect from them when they come into the studio? How prepared do you expect them to be?"

"I see."

"That way you still retain control, you get to offer your services as a favor and you both end up with something valuable. You only need to do that so many times before you've built up a portfolio, and at that point you can start charging every new band that comes in."

"That...that actually makes sense," Casey said. Noah's logic showed promise and Casey started coming around to his way of thinking.

"It's much easier to get started if you lead with a giving mindset. If you give first, people often reciprocate with gifts of their own as a form of repayment."

"You get what you give?" Casey asked.

"Yes, as the New Radicals would say," Noah answered and laughed.

"It's easier to find clients to build a portfolio because you remove the conversation about money until you're confident about your worth. It also eliminates some of the barriers to entry into the music community because you're not bringing up money all the time. You'll get to know the music scene much faster because you won't be actively soliciting them. If you tell them upfront that you'll do your work for free in exchange for something that you need, in this case a portfolio item, it makes the conversation easier." Noah sliced off a piece of his pancake while Casey dipped his sashimi in his Wasabi-filled soy sauce dish.

"It opens up a much better conversation than leading with money," Noah said with his mouth full.

"What do you mean?" Casey asked.

Noah swallowed his pancake and continued, "Like we talked about last weekend. You need to focus on impact instead of costs. You want to ask the band about the goals for the recordings. What do they hope to achieve with their records? How are they going to use them? What doors will an album open for them? Are they hoping to sell their record, or use it as a calling card on streaming services? What is the album worth to them in the long run? The more questions you ask, the better you understand the reasoning behind their desire to record. The more you understand your customer, the better your relationship with them will be. It will also show that you care. The person who asks the best questions wins because they care so much more about understanding how they can help. You aren't just somebody who's getting a job. You're the person solving a problem for them."

"The person who asks the best questions?" Casey repeated Noah's statement, confused.

"Ah yes, the Socratic method of constantly asking questions. Your impact comes from the quality of the questions you ask. The beautiful thing about the Socratic method is that if you ask more questions than you make statements, you'll learn more about other people, in this case your potential clients," Noah stated. "And the better questions you ask, the wiser you become."

Casey chuckled at Noah's statements because he hardly ever asked any questions. It was ironic, but what Casey needed at this moment was food for thought, not more questions to answer.

Casey thought back to how simply rewriting the copy on his website using his understanding of what he thought his customer needed had helped him land last week's gig. The mindset shift of thinking about his business from the client's point of view instead of his own was a valuable lesson. Noah looked over Casey's shoulder. He pointed to a poster of a local band that was set to play the following weekend. As Casey turned around, an octave-pedal solo wailed a series of bends that crashed into the final chorus of Weezer's "Buddy Holly" overhead.

"Take this band, for example. If they're thinking selfishly about themselves and how they deserve gigs because people *need to hear their music*, that's a difficult value proposition to bring to whatever venue they want to play at."

"How so?" Casey asked, not clear on where Noah was going with his digression.

"They're not solving a problem for the venue. The bar owner isn't booking the band out of the goodness of their heart. They're not booking a band because they think their music is great, *even if they do like the band*."

"Why are they booking them then?"

"They're booking the band because the bar owner has a *revenue problem they think a band can help with*. You get booked at bars because you draw a crowd, are easy to work with, or play great music. If you have two of those qualities you'll get booked again. If you have all three, you're golden! But the most important part of that triangle is drawing a crowd because the venue's goal is to *make money*."

Casey frowned, trying to put Noah's point into perspective. How did Trailer Trash Tendencies get a gig? They did draw a crowd so they had that going for them. Their music wasn't awful, even though they couldn't perform in the studio, so they had that going for them too. Maybe they were nice to the booking agent, even if they weren't great to work with in the studio. Casey put the pointless thought out of his mind. The venue was terribly managed anyway, no need to analyze it further.

Noah sighed and pushed his food away. "The purpose of a business is to solve a problem for an audience that has it. In this case, the bar's problem is an empty cash register at the end of the night. It's meeting payroll at the end of the month. If a band can position itself as helping fill up the venue so that the bar makes money, that's a way easier sell than demanding to get stage time."

Noah's explanation made complete sense to Casey. "So I should position my services as someone who is helping my customers solve a problem I know they have, that I know I can help them with?"

"Exactly," Noah said. "Having an impact-driven, results-oriented approach to solving your customers' problems puts you on a higher level than some random Craigslist poster looking for a job."

"Like Buttrock Barry," Casey said and chuckled, remembering their conversation from last week.

"Like Buttrock Barry," Noah repeated and laughed. "Because you're just starting out, you might think you need to race to the bottom and cut your prices because of all the Buttrock Barrys who charge $5/hour or $50/project. But those guys won't ever last because their math doesn't add up.

"Their math?" Casey asked.

"Business is a math problem, and once you think about it that way you start to see the possibilities you have available. But Craigslist Larry and Buttrock Barry never thought about the unsustainability of their business model."

Casey looked at Noah like a cow looks at an oncoming train. Math now? He was barely warming up to the idea of understanding how marketing could be a bearable part of his job, but now he needed to know math too?

Noah pressed on, "Let me give you an example. If you're charging $5 per hour and you fill out the average work year, which is about 2,080 hours, you'll make $10,400 a year. That's less than minimum wage and it won't help your career at all. It leaves no room for investing in your business. It hardly even gives you money to eat ramen, let alone have lunch at a real Japanese restaurant," Noah waved his arms around, expressing their location and making his point. "I don't think you want to start a business so you can go back to living like a poor college student, right?"

Casey shook his head, "No, I've had my fair share of pasta and ramen thank you very much."

"Right," Noah continued. "Even if you land enough clients to work on a 10-song album every month you'll only make $6,000 in a year at $50 per song, so you can easily see how it's a losing proposition. There's simply no way you can make a livable career out of that. Let's say it takes you eight hours to get to a finished mix when you just start out. Even if you were to work every weekday and finish one song every day, that's only $13,000 a year, and you don't even get a vacation or a single day off. Sounds like an exhausting career to me."

"Yeah, not exactly the fun I thought I would be having," Casey said dejectedly.

"And here's where your hourly rate really gets you into trouble. Let me ask you: if all of a sudden it only took you two hours to finish a project because you gained the experience necessary to become more efficient, do you think you should lower your rate to $10 per project because *you* are more efficient?"

Casey hesitated, never having thought about it in those terms.

"No, of course not," Noah answered for him. "That would be ridiculous. You should benefit from your efficiency. And it goes both ways too. Once you become more efficient and gain more experience, chances are your projects end up sounding better."

Casey nodded and ate the last of his sushi roll while Noah continued his monologue. "Severed" by the Decemberists blasted as loud as a song could blast out of a quiet restaurant speaker system. This was, after all, like one of those scenes in the movies where it was perfectly reasonable to hear both parties in a conversation over loud and thumping club beats.

"The value of your hour includes all the experience and education you have accumulated, not just what you're doing for the client at that moment. That's why you can't be charging minimum wage for projects. The combined value of your hour is way higher than the value of an entry-level employee making minimum wage. You're trying to make a bigger impact by offering high-end professional services. You're not just a pawn of a peon working at a check-in counter somewhere."

Casey could agree to that logic. It had taken him a long time to hone his skills, and although they were already pretty good, understanding the mathematical specifics of pricing made things so much clearer and logical.

"What do you do when you do a full project for a band?" Noah asked.

"I record, edit, and mix their songs," Casey said.

"Sure, but if you had to break it down, what was the expertise you used?"

Casey thought about everything he did during the last recording session and the skills he used instinctively to run it smoothly. "Well, understanding signal flow. Feel for rhythm and timing. Understanding of digital signal processors like EQ and compression."

"And what else?"

"Well, when I recorded that first band, I coaxed the musicians to be in their best mood for the performance. I remember taking a break because things seemed to be going south, and with a quick breather we went back in and knocked it out," Casey said, telling a version of the story that didn't include his most annoying frustrations.

"So, what you're saying is that you *wasted* a part of an hour to regroup so you could save time in the long run while making sure the performance was more impactful and of higher quality than it would have been if you tried to make fit within that hour?" Noah asked in a run-on sentence.

"Yes. I suppose so."

"That's a great reason for making sure you charge on value instead of hours. Charge for impactful results. You were using psychology, empathy, and intuition to make the session go smoothly. That's more important than making every second of every hour count in some arbitrary way. Your value is not in hours, it is in the impact of the final result."

Casey nodded, "So if I'm doing a mix, it's the quality and impact that matters, not the amount of time I put in?"

"Exactly," Noah said. "Say you get a recorded song that has all sorts of problems, so it takes you longer than usual to mix. But along the way you learn some techniques to tackle the situations if they ever arise again. When you get another recording to mix that has similar problems, but now you can tackle them swiftly and cut out hours of your time, does that mean you should charge less?"

Casey shook his head, "Of course not. My value has increased because I'm more efficient."

"That's right. After a while you may create efficiencies in your workflow that make you even faster. That just makes you more valuable. If you still charge hourly, your value to yourself goes down. Do you see how that works against you?"

Casey was starting to get it, "The more efficient I am, the better it is for everyone and the bigger impact I can make with the same hours that everyone else has."

"Exactly, your hours have gotten more valuable. And if you have a quality product, you're able to raise your rates because you've learned new ways to solve problems your clients don't know how to fix. Now, let's say you raise your rates to $200 per project and it only takes you two hours to complete. That means you're now making $100 per hour. So instead of working more hours for low pay, you're now working fewer hours with the same results. And the *results* are what make the clients happy. If you're undercharging, there is an immediate suspicion of whether you're good enough. But when you actually charge in the ballpark of what you're worth, you get taken more seriously. You may not get every gig because there will always be people who are looking for the cheapest option, but you don't want to work with those people anyway."

Casey kept reliving his first nightmare client and was determined to keep those cases to a minimum. The thought of working with bands like that again sent shivers down his spine.

"And here's when the math starts working out," Noah continued. "Now, if you're doing a single project every day at $200 per project, but only working two hours, you not only make $52,000 a year but you also have six extra working hours every day devoted to *growing your business.* Do you see how much better of a career that is? You have more flexibility. You can take days off. You can invest in yourself because you're not overworking yourself in this race to the bottom."

Noah's way of doing business made way more sense the more Casey thought about it. They finished up their lunch and parted ways for the day, with Casey having a lot to think about.

SUCCESS STRATEGY #3
BE A PROBLEM-SOLVER

Businesses exist to solve problems. Businesses succeed when they focus on solving a problem for their customers. What are you hoping to solve for your ideal customer? If you are constantly searching for what problems you can solve for your potential customers, you will always be putting their needs first and they will feel like you are taking care of them.

Download the Success Strategies worksheets at www.YouGetWhatYouGiveBook.com and start solving problems for your clients that helps you make your business math add up.

CHAPTER 9
SUCCESS LIKELY

Noah's perspective made Casey think about his fledgling studio business in a completely different way. He now understood how his impact was calculated on the combined experience he had to offer, not the hours he worked. Figuring out how to view his studio as a business that solved problems was trickier, but he knew that the reason most musicians use recording engineers and producers was so that they can focus on making the music without worrying about the technical part. It dawned on Casey that positioning his studio in such a way would make it clearer to his clients exactly how he would help them make an impact. Casey was helping them save time because his clients could delegate all the work to him so that they could focus on what they did best.

The next day he got a call from Sam, an old music buddy he hadn't seen in years. Sam was in Scam Likely, an ironically named power pop trio that played catchy and quick songs people could jump up and down to as they shouted the simple lyrics to their choruses. They were working on an EP and it wasn't going so well.

"We got a good deal from a producer, but I should've known it was too good to be true," Sam told Casey. Now they were stuck with bad demos and nowhere to go.

Sam had seen Casey's Facebook posts about opening his studio business and reached out to him to see whether he could help his band out of the hole they had dug for themselves. *I guess they got tired of scraping the bottom of the barrel with Buttrock Barry.* Casey drilled them with questions so he could understand them better. He wanted to know as much about their project as possible. Once he understood exactly what they were after, he put a detailed proposal together that listed everything that he would do to help them succeed.

The band got excited about the professional way in which Casey handled himself and they jumped at the offer to get started. They sent him rehearsal recordings ahead of time so he was familiar with the songs. He made notes on the arrangement of certain songs that he thought could be tightened up and hoped they would be open to his direction. He loved the band's demos and was excited to help them create a great product for their career.

Although Casey didn't understand the first thing about being a producer, the simple vision of making something valuable and worth an impact was all the guidance he needed. He had read enough interviews with famous producers to know that everybody did it differently, so he had an informed confidence that he could find his role during the session. Besides, nobody ever really knew what they were doing. They gained their skills through experience. Pushing himself out of his comfort zone was the action he needed to make at this moment to get to the next level.

Once again, Casey was prepared for the recording session and to his relief the band seemed confident and ready to rock. When Sam and the gang came in, they were nothing but professionals. Casey was ready with all the equipment that they needed to get started. Compared to Trailer Trash Tendencies, these guys were pros, like a beautifully remastered lossless vinyl record compared to a hyper-compressed, 64 kbps mp3 that was uploaded to YouTube.

They set up their instruments and amps while Casey miked them up. Mics on every drum, with two each on the kick and snare. Overheads placed in a spaced pair angled slightly off from the edge of the cymbals to get a smoother sound. With a quick thwack on the snare, he could position the mics in phase with each other, avoiding the annoying high-end swoosh an out-of-phase kit makes. Casey then added a room mic to capture the overall kit before he turned to the guitar and bass. He decided to keep it simple with a Shure SM57 on the guitar amp and a DI box for the bass. Sam's amp sounded good in the room so he had no worries about whether the tone would translate to the recording and the DI'd bass could always be manipulated and tweaked with various amp simulators and modelers to get the tone the songs needed. Casey placed a few baffles around the guitar amp to minimize bleed going into the drum mics and was relieved that he didn't have to worry about giant bass tones clouding up the drum recording.

Once everyone was ready the drummer counted into the first song. If they ever had red-light fever, they had long since lost track of their temperature. They knew their songs inside and out and could play off each other like a touring band that had lived and breathed their songs each day for the last year. The band performed as a whole and flowed together through the song. Not with army-accurate, robotic-grid consistency, but as an organism.

The typical robotically edited performance you would hear on some of the modern hits had the undesirable effect of sucking out all sense of feel and performance, locking them together in a rhythmic prison instead of a flowing dance. These guys were different. Besides, musicians don't ever play locked to a grid, no matter how well the drummer can keep time with the click track. There's always a natural weaving around the beat that happens when three human beings musically feed off each other.

The bass player kept a constant groove, a fraction of a note in front of the kick drum to propel the music forward with excitement. The guitar player laid back on his rhythm, locking in with the hi-hat and playing slightly behind the beat, adding an additional layer to the groove.

The trio took their respective positions within the beat and the excitement of the song was electrifying. Each person had their own private pocket to groove within, tied to the other players' performance. The groove was tight while flamming just right. Being in the same room as such an incredible rock band made Casey completely forget about all of his troubles for the time being. Inside a moment of musical amazingness there is no outside world. No other plans on the schedule. No other worries to think about. Casey even forgot how much money he had left in his savings account. The only thing that mattered to him at that moment was that he knew it was exactly where he wanted to be. His only focus was the music pummeling his ears from his closed-back monitoring headphones.

The trio quickly laid down the rhythm tracks for the EP. They recorded a few passes of each of the four songs on the EP and then gathered around Casey to listen back.

"I like the last take of Dirty Harriet," Sam said, his tone commanding leadership while still feeling open to suggestions. "Dirty Harriet" was without a doubt the first single from this EP, they had decided. It was a tongue-in-cheek social commentary on police brutality in black America with an infectiously catchy chorus Casey had seen them play live. The narrator in the 3-minute song, a female cop taking on the "blue rotten apples," was the typical merging of pop culture references and social issues Sam found important. The chorus was a simple masterpiece of the call and response variety, with Sam screaming "Do you feel lucky!" and his bandmates responding, "Punk!" It killed it live when the audience joined in, the entire venue yelling "punk!" at the top of their lungs, bodies bouncing up and down, hands thrust into the air, fingers crossed in the reverse Spidey web-fluid formation of Rock 'n' Roll.

"I think I hit a wrong note in the last chorus," Alex, the bass player, said.

Casey quickly solo'd the bass track and listened intently to the raunchy riffing of Alex's playing. Sure enough, halfway through the final chorus an odd note appeared. Casey was a ninja at editing so he quickly found the same part in a previous take, chopped up the note and pasted it over the pesky fart. A few quick crossfades later, the take was topped and trimmed with no one the wiser. Casey unsolo'd the track and played the final chorus for the boys who nodded along.

"You're good at this," Sam said, his lower lip sticking out in satisfaction.

"Hey, you guys make it easy for me," Casey replied.

The band broke for lunch while Casey edited the rest of the songs. Although the band was really tight, there were occasional spots in the groove where the pocket felt too large so he quickly tightened up any odd spots that felt loose. Casey wanted to make sure that all the overdubs were recorded to as tight of a rhythm track as possible because it was the only way to keep the songs from falling apart. Music is about excitement and emotion and Casey's job as a producer was to transfer the musician's emotions into the tracks they were recording.

When the band came back, they got ready for overdubs. While they found the right tone for the second rhythm guitar track, Casey said, "Hey Sam, let's do a quick vocal first, just to get a take without any of the bleed from the drums."

He already had a scratch vocal track but he had a feeling Sam could overanalyze his vocal performance. Casey knew the vocal was the most important part of any song and there was intense pressure, both on him and Sam to nail that vocal. Sam was already warmed up from singing all the scratch vocals so Casey thought that taking the pressure off would make Sam more comfortable.

Sam shrugged, "Ok," and started to take his guitar off his shoulder.

"Just leave the guitar on, we're just doing this take for fun to see how it sounds without bleed from the rest of the instruments."

Casey knew that Sam was more comfortable singing and playing guitar at the same time, so he made sure that even though the guitar wasn't plugged in it could serve as a safety blanket for additional comfort and confidence.

Case knew that if the recording become "just for fun," it would lead to a better performance. Taking the pressure off was key to a better take. Casey quickly dialed in some reverb and parallel compression on

Sam's vocal so that he could feel like he was singing to a record instead of a demo.

Three minutes later, Sam opened his eyes as if he was coming back from another world and said, "Damn, that felt great!" Casey nodded and let out a sly smile, knowing for a fact that there was no beating that take. He knew that if he would give Sam the opportunity to second-guess himself, he'd screw up by overthinking it.

Producing music was so much more than just setting up a studio to record and finding the right plug-ins to make a good mix. It's about creating a vibe and leading the musicians in the right direction. Sometimes you don't tell them what they're doing, and sometimes you need to put blinders on them while you lead the way. Other times, being an engineer is just pushing buttons with the right band in the room and you're just lucky enough to put your name on it.

CHAPTER 10
IMPOSTER SYNDROME

"**W**ould you like to hear what's new?" the robot asked him.

"No, play music," Noah responded.

"Motorcycle Drive By" faded up through the speakers as he moved from the kitchen to his studio. The guitars plucked a clean arpeggio before Stephan Jenkins' vocals entered.

The first thing Noah stopped paying attention to was the news. He was happier that way. It caused him nothing but anxiety, which got in the way of his creative work.

It used to be that he'd check the newspaper first thing in the morning, then it became a computer dashboard. Then finally, the phone shackled to his bed. Whether it was one more negative news story, or an angry email from some random person who found him online, it took him long enough to realize that nothing positive came out of checking his phone first thing in the morning.

So he deleted the apps that destroyed his clarity. He removed the knee-jerk habit of rolling on his side to grab his phone, one shoulder underneath him, the other arm shaped like a hook, his fingers holding the bait of whatever would derail his day. Instead, routine and planning; the mindset of intentionality replaced the reactionary mindlessness of seeing what the world was screaming about every morning.

So it was yesterday, and so it will be tomorrow. All of this has happened before and will happen again, he learned from his nephew's favorite TV show, Battlestar Galactica, a sci-fi epic he enjoyed immensely. Although it had painted a bleak cycle for humanity's inevitable rise and fall, and rise again, there was also the glimmer of hope from "All Along the Watchtower" that had a recurring musical cameo throughout the series. And he thought, *there must be some kind of way out of here*, and through repetition, deliberate practice, mindful productivity and most importantly, serving others, he had found a way to make an impact with his life.

He learned at any early age that a dead-end job was never going to be for him. So, he had set out to learn everything he could about music so he could help make the world feel more emotionally connected. Business degree with a minor in music. Internship at various music magazines. Becoming a staff writer at Rolling Stone in his twenties. Becoming a music producer with his own independent label in his late thirties. A string of hits, honors, accolades and accomplishments.

Ennui ensued after that while he misguidedly chased the yellow brick road for more money instead of savoring the experiences and the art that really mattered. He always thought he needed to have a certain amount so that he could do the things he needed in order to become the person he wanted to be. It wasn't until later that he realized that the math was backward. You must first decide to become who you want to be and then do the things that type of person does in order to get and have the things you want. Your destiny is made manifest in your mind and it is only controlled by you. Not by some invisible force or random chance, but by you making purposeful choices to put into the world what you want to make happen.

The second thing to go: social media. Social media was addictive, but he was sober. The endless scroll through a picture-perfect landscape of humans he knew were faking it did not impress him.

He understood the allure of using marketing for promotion, but too often the marketing was so fake it destroyed any good intention the brands set out to create. He respected the immense psychological pull of social media and how it gave its users little shots of dopamine to keep the user coming back for more. How addictive it was to be social, yet how alone you could feel in the world of make-believe filters and flawless photography. He figured that if you used marketing to persuade and entice without any exchange of real value, you were no better than a drug dealer peddling dime bags in a dark alley.

Jenkins sang in the background about people careening through the universe without stopping and it was a perfect analogy for the endless scroll that stops people from building something of value. The band worked its way toward the inevitable crescendo of the greatest breakup song in the world.

In the grand scheme of things, social media had little impact. It was fickle and fleeting. Messages were ignored by 98% of scrollers and any value a post had could vanish with the flick of a thumb. Self-promotion had its place, but only if the underlying value was created from a place of integrity with the intention to exchange value in such a way that empowered both parties to level up.

Noah had accounts, posted rarely and never scrolled the feed. His students would argue about the importance of promoting their work through social media, and to a certain extent, he agreed. However, it only extended to the point where it interfered with meaningful work that made an impact in people's lives.

Social media was useless unless you had a system in place to help you deliver impact in your customers' lives. If you could create a master key system behind it that delivered the clients his students wanted, he could tolerate the machine, even if he deemed it unnecessary.

Instead, he focused on deep work. Work that moved the needle. Uninterrupted creative time to make things that mattered. He knew that big things came in small, incremental improvements of challenging yourself to be 4% better than you were the day before.

The song softly concluded, hopeful and melancholic all at once. The weird withdrawal symptoms from social media had made him feel more alone for a while, but after he got over it, he felt more alive than ever.

Alone, away from the perfectly crafted posts of people who should use their time for something more meaningful he turned to his writing. His writing corner was tidy because he couldn't have it any other way. How could he organize his thoughts if he couldn't organize the room they would emerge from? The laptop sat by his chair, the natural light from his window illuminating the room. If music production was about creating a vibe with dim lights, lava lamps and carpets, writing was about creating an enlightened and brilliant ambience in which your thoughts would feel welcome to come out.

Noah, like all creatives, was stuck with an imaginary friend he never asked for. He called his imaginary imposter within Janus. He had learned to live with him ever since he started following his creative impulses. Even if he knew his thoughts were only for journaling, the inner imposter still had to be coaxed away with sunlight and warmth.

When thoughts were meant for publishing however, Janus would grow even stronger and throw a fit, questioning everything in their vicinity. Now, his room not only had to be perfectly set up and organized, but the timing had to be perfect too. If even so much as a minute would misalign in their routine, the imposter within skulked around Noah's mind, fussing about how *the writing's no good today and we should probably just try again tomorrow.*

"It's time for a break anyway," Janus would say.

"After only five minutes?" Noah would laugh.

Janus hated finishing but he loved to start a new project. The closer to finishing a creative work, the louder Janus got. Predictably, he was always more critical of the current work that was nearing completion, while filled with ideas and opportunities for what they could achieve in the future. Some new and exciting, yet distant, project that was sure to bring them both the happiness they needed.

Noah had learned to live with the imposter within. He called him Janus after the two-headed god of beginnings and transitions, simultaneously looking into the past and the future yet never really focused on the present. But Noah knew that the present was where the work needed to happen so he fought the battle every day.

He knew everyone carried a version of Janus in their mind, like a distorted mutation of "Footsteps in the Sand," where the second pair of footprints kept you from your potential the entire time except for the short path where you were able to shake off the fear long enough to publish your work.

Noah knew that putting your work out there was terrifying, but the thing about fear was that once you faced it, it would dissolve in a plume of smoke, like an optical illusion. Not putting yourself out there was even worse. It meant giving up before even trying, allowing a figment of your imagination to win the battle before you ever started the first round. He knew that the only people who succeeded were the ones who took action. It was walking the walk that got you to your destination. Buying the Lonely Planet guide just to tell people how excited you are about traveling to a destination to which you'd never buy a ticket wouldn't get you anywhere. Noah didn't know how many times he'd advised someone that things didn't have to be perfect—only good enough. Good enough was good enough until you were good enough to be better. That only came from continuously putting yourself out there and improving along the way, challenging yourself to practice in public because it was the only arena that mattered.

He kept a writing practice to keep his mind sharp. He had kept the writing habit for as long as he could remember. Most of his writings were journal entries never to be enjoyed by anyone except himself—but many made their way onto his blog in some form or another. Other times he would write the occasional article for a magazine that hired him based on past accomplishments.

He would write a book every now and then for the fans that still followed him, but he looked at his writing like he viewed anything: as a habit that would inevitably bleed into other aspects of his life. Writing down his thoughts helped manifest them so that he could understand himself better.

Sharing his story helped other people understand what he stood for, where he was coming from and how he could help. Providing useful information that could help his students was the easiest way for him to make an impact, and sharing his story was a crucial pillar of his success. The only way he could create relationships with his audience was to share his story because it was the only way they could understand him enough to be able to relate. If nobody knew your story, how could they relate to you and decide whether you were the person to help them out?

He remembered his friend Arnór, an Icelandic music journalist that had taken him on a tour of the Icelandic music scene a few years back, showing him all the old haunts, dives, and concert houses that gave a platform to some of the greatest Icelandic artists in history: The Sugarcubes, Björk, Of Monsters and Men, Sigur Rós, Múm, Mugison, Árstíðir, Þursaflokkurinn (and their more popular twin Stuðmenn), Emilíana Torrini and Páll Óskar. Noah had furthered his research into Icelandic music and came across some lesser-known acts outside of its shores that were equally amazing: Ensími, Megas, Mínus, Vicky, Agent Fresco, Dikta, Sign, Botnleðja, Lay Low, Pétur Ben, Jónas Sig, Dr. Spock, Quarashi, Fjallabræður and Hjálmar. For such a small country it seemed like an endless well of talent.

The journalist told him that the Icelandic word for

customer or client was the consonant-crazed, marble-mouthed word "Viðskiptavinur." He further explained that the word was derived from two root words, "viðskipti" the word for business, and "vinur" the word for friend. So, it seemed that in Iceland, possibly because of the small population and the fact that word-of-mouth travels fast when there are not that many mouths, it would behoove you to become friends with your customers as much as possible. This resonated with Noah because what is business other than a trans-action where both parties exchange value in such a way that both are better off?

After Noah's musical tour of Reykjavík they joined up with a friend of Arnór's. Over drinks at an oddly named nightclub called Sódóma Reykjavík, a name Noah chuckled at, they shared the quirks of their language.

"Did you know that the word stupidity comes from the Latin word "stupere" which means to be numb or astounded?" Sigurður, Icelandic Wool-Sweater-Wear-ing Chap #1, asked in the hard and bright accent that staccatoed in a dotted rhythm with the accent on the one and three.

"I did," Noah said, nodding in agreement.

Arnór chimed in as if they were tagging each other out in a call and response fashion like old bandmates, "In Icelandic, the word for stupidity is 'heimska.' It's derived from the word 'heim,' meaning 'home.' It's originally from Old Norse, 'heimskr.'"

Sigurður smiled with satisfaction and mock superiority, "In Old Norse, 'heimskr' meant that you were foolish and silly because you had never sailed away from home. To us, it means staying home, refusing to learn about new things happening over the horizon from your farm."

Sigurður, who turned out to have a Master's degree from the University of Iceland in both the Icelandic language and Human Development, continued, "Personally, I like the idea that our language tells us that staying home will make you dumb. You won't learn anything new and you'll end up a naive ignoramus that refuses knowledge."

"It's a bit ironic that a nation of 350,000 people stuck on an island in the North Atlantic believe this. It's not like it's the easiest place to set out to explore from," Noah joked.

Arnór got immediately animated in the way Icelanders do when they're passionate. He quickly put his beer down and waved his finger above his head, "But that's *why* it's so great our language reminds us in this way. It's *because* it's harder that makes it all the more important."

Arnór, the calmer of the bunch, crossed his legs and zipped down his own wool sweater, the warmth of the bar too hot for a sweater designed to protect you in freezing temperatures. He opined in a scholarly fashion, "Well...although we are technically stuck on an island, our ancestors were... well, let's call them 'zealous travelers.' The Vikings discovered 'America' first."

"Before quickly forgetting about it again!" Sigurður chimed in with his finger still aloft.

"They raided random parts of Europe. They even had settlements as far south as Sicily. So, ignoring the whole bloodshed and sweeping it under the wool rug in a way," Arnór made a sweeping motion with a guilty shrug on his face.

"Yes, there is the whole raiding, raping and pillaging thing I'm afraid," Sigurður said, having resumed a calm posture cleaning his glasses with his shirt. "I think we've evolved from that. There is no crime here compared to other countries, and there are almost no murders." He held his spectacles in front of his face and exhaled into the lens.

"The Vikings discovered things they realized they could never have known if they had stayed home. Staying home does not teach you anything real about the world," Sigurður said in absolutes. "Researching can shed some light on the subjects you wish to know more about, but it is no substitute for living and immersing yourself in other cultures and countries where you can further your education about the world."

"The same could be said about your comfort zone. If you never get out of your comfort zone or try new things, you won't learn anything new," Noah stated.

"Exactly!" Arnór said, "If you don't travel, you won't experience other countries or cultures. The best-case scenario is that you'll end up being a bit boring and won't have much to add to the conversation."

"The worst-case scenario is that you'll end up a racist xenophobe," Sigurður added.

Noah preferred neither. He learned that day that avoiding "heimska" can also lead to increased creativity. To be creative was to be open to new creative opportunities. The only way to create unique things was through mixing a few different things together.

Mix writing and drawing together to create graphic novels. Mix photography and painting and the world gets Mixed Media. Mix old swing records from the 1930s with electronic dance music and out pops something like Parov Stelar, the Electro Swing group from Austria. Although simple examples, creative combinations are endless.

Noah knew that in order to grow, you had to learn. Yet the more he learned, the less he seemed to know because he realized just how much more knowledge was out there in the world.

So this morning Noah wrote (with Janus stubbornly silent by his side) about how the opposite of stupidity was not wisdom. Rather, it was the willingness to learn. Although staying stupid was easier, it was still an action whether it was conscious or not. The absence of action through inaction was still a decision. *By not taking the action of being open to new things,* he wrote, *you're taking the action of staying stupid. If you strive to push the boundaries of your comfort zone, try new things and learn new skills, you'll grow wise.*

Noah strived to encourage this thinking in his students. The paradigm shift was easy enough because expanding your horizons should be a no-brainer. For the music industry professionals that he mentored, he always recommended studying the genres in which they were *not* experts in, exploring new sounds or discovering new artists like he did during his vacation in Iceland.

He found that no accomplished artist was happy staying stagnant because it led to ennui and complacency.

He finished for the day, writing, *if you get out of your comfort zone and learn new skills along the way, you'll grow in creative ways you never thought possible. See your creative potential as a vast ocean and yourself as the Viking explorer, sailing away from your creative home base and expanding your creative potential along the way.*

SUCCESS STRATEGY #4
FOCUS ON DEEP WORK AND AVOID
DISTRACTIONS

Remember the last time you ended a workday and said to yourself, "man, I felt like I was working hard all day, but I didn't really feel like I did anything." Not all tasks are created equal.

Most work falls into one of two categories:

1. Deep and impactful creative work
2. Scattered and shallow busywork

Eliminate the latter as much as possible. These are usually "little tweaks" that are unnecessary. Reviewing stats, "planning" instead of "doing," or just refreshing your email inbox so you can tackle something meaningless instead of doing the deep work that's necessary. It's the equivalent of walking around the office with a stack of papers that you're taking nowhere in particular. Just imagine how many hours you could free up to work on your creative projects if you eliminated the busywork from your life.

Deep and impactful creative work is the only type of work that moves the needle and brings you closer to your goals. Work that has intention will make an impact. Prioritize impact, eliminate busywork. Schedule your time for deep, intentional and impactful work. Put it on your calendar and show up for it. Give it the respect it deserves. Follow through with your plan.

Find out more about doing work that matters at
www.YouGetWhatYouGiveBook.com

CHAPTER 11
WHO'S YOUR FRIEND?

The following weekend Casey got a text from Noah, telling him to meet for lunch at Medici's, a fast-casual pizza place in the middle of the arts district. When he arrived at Medici's, Noah was already there, joined by a cool looking rock chick with white hair who looked strangely familiar. When Noah saw Casey in the doorway, he motioned for him to come over and join them. The organ of "One Headlight" by The Wallflowers floated through the air as he made his way over to the duo.

"Casey, I want you to meet my friend Amie."

"I think I know who you are, I've seen your ads online right? It's very nice to meet you!" Casey exclaimed and shook Amie's hand.

Noah interrupted, "Yes, Amie is the content queen of the internet. She's built quite the session-drumming business for herself that way."

"Noah tells me that you're trying to build a music business of your own, is it?"

"Yes, I'm a recording engineer and producer. Or at least, I hope to be if I could get some clients in the door."

Noah chuckled, "Well that's why I thought I'd bring Amie along today, because she's got quite the hang of finding clients all over the world. But first, let's order lunch! I'm starving."

They each ordered a personal pie from the counter. Medici's was famous for its alternative concoctions and odd combinations of flavors. Amie ordered the Pesto Chicken, Noah ordered the White Mediterranean and Casey debated between the Angry Samoan BBQ and the Steak and Blue Cheese pizza, finally settling on the BBQ.

As they sat back down with their lunch Amie asked Casey, "So what kind of clients do you work with now?"

"I'm trying to work with anyone that wants to make a record," Casey stated.

"Just anyone...?" Noah fished.

Casey chuckled, "Well, not everyone. At first it was anyone who needed anything, but now I'm trying to find good clients that are willing to believe in their music enough to make an impact."

Noah turned to Amie, "Who are your clients Amie?"

"I work mostly with singer/songwriters who are doing things independently. Specifically, guitarists who are serious about their music and want to release it, but need drums because they either can't play the drums themselves, or simply don't have any connections with drummers who could help them out."

Casey was impressed with the specificity of Amie's answer and now couldn't help but wonder how lacking his own description was. Noah smiled and nodded along with Amie's description as she continued, "Bands are rarely interested in working with me because they usually have their own drummer, so that would be redundant." Amie rolled her eyes and laughed.

"So you work specifically with singer/songwriters?" Casey asked.

"Yes, or often it's like a half-band sorta situation where there are maybe two core members and neither of them play the drums, but they both want a fully fleshed out sound on their records. They're invested in making their music the best it can be."

"So, your customer isn't just everyone?" Noah pried.

Amie gave Noah a knowing look and laughed, "What a leading question! No, I focus on finding the clients that have vision and are trying to bring their music to the next level, but because they live in a rural area, or don't know any drummers, they turn to me as the best alternative. I'm selling a service that elevates their music to the next level. My clients hire me because they know I have both the experience, the gear, and the understanding of what they're trying to achieve."

"Wow, that's very specific," Casey said.

"Just one of the lessons I learned from our guy over

here," Amie cocked her head in Noah's direction and chuckled.

"One of the worst things you can assume when you're starting your business is to think that "everyone" can be your customer. Disqualifying your prospects and deciding who you're *not* for is equally important as finding the right client you want to work with," Noah said.

"So, you reject work if they don't fit who you want to work with?" Casey asked.

Noah motioned to Amie, who picked up his thread, "There are certainly clients I won't work with. Not because the client isn't serious, but for certain genres I'm just not the right drummer for them. I only feel comfortable playing certain music and if I don't think I can do it justice for them, then I shouldn't just do it because of the money."

"It doesn't help you make an impact?" Casey asked.

"Exactly. It doesn't help me help the client make the most out of their music. At that point I usually just refer them to somebody else."

"Aren't you worried that you're just giving business away?"

"I think whatever I give away comes back in a generous way."

"I'd be worried that people would try to steal business away from me," Casey admitted.

"What I offer and what my competition offers are two different things," Amie continued. "Some are selling drum tracks for the lowest price. I put myself into the project as an invaluable member of the team who helps them realize their vision. I spend more time getting to understand their music. That's something a random Craigslist drummer can't do, and something a programmed drum loop can't either. I'm positioning myself as a temporary member of their band. I'm not trying to earn an extra dollar by trying to get as many drum tracking sessions as possible."

"But what if they immediately ask about money?"

"When a client comes to me and immediately starts talking about money, I try to steer the conversation into what they want to achieve with their music."

"So, you ask questions?" Casey asked, remembering his previous lunch with Noah and how he recommended digging into his clients' pains and fears, and hopes and dreams.

Amie nodded, "Of course, they may have a budget in mind, but more often than not they're clueless about how to do any of this stuff, so they need a leader to help them realize their vision. That's where your understanding of the entire process comes in. If you immediately give them an hourly rate, what do you think they're thinking of?"

"What's the least amount of hours they need?" Casey answered and Noah mocked an imaginary bell ringing the correct answer.

"That's right, but unfortunately, that's the wrong question. The right question is: *what's the best work of art I can create at this moment in my career,* and that's a hard thing to help musicians understand who are only thinking about the cheapest option they can find. By focusing on adding value and creating impact, you set yourself apart from the hawks circling the scene looking to poach people's clients. You don't want *just anybody*. You want to fit in with them so you can join them on their journey. It's a blessing to eliminate clients who can't be your customer because it helps you focus on who really matters—people you can really help."

Amie took another bite of her pizza while she let her last point sit in the air. Casey chewed on Amie's point. Amie and Noah were obviously good friends as they shared slices with each other, trying out each other's order and maximizing their enjoyment.

"Yeah, I'm just starting to understand how to think about all this stuff…" Before Casey could finish his sentence, Amie finished his thought for him, "but the more you understand, the less you know?"

"Exactly!" Casey exclaimed and Noah nodded along with them.

"So how did you figure out what to charge for your services?" Casey asked Amie.

"My initial approach was, 'I have no idea how much I should be charging because I am new to this, and I don't know,'" Amie laughed.

"That sounds familiar!" Casey cried.

"So, I initially started by asking people to pay whatever they want or whatever they can just to get an idea of the ballpark."

Casey remembered Noah's advice on doing free

work as a way of establishing his worth and how Amie's approach was just a variation of the theme.

Amie continued, "And I've just gradually been sort of raising my rate from there as my skills have gotten better. And as my equipment has been upgraded and, you know, I've spent a lot of money on investing in my business."

"Money you get from charging a valuable rate that leaves money available to invest in growing your business," Noah interjected.

"That's right. And remember, Casey, your clients only care about their music, not what *you want to invest in*. They expect you to have the equipment necessary to get *them* results. But you still have to care about investing in yourself in order to get better results. That's why it's so important to find clients who will also support that. And remember that if you're charging the bottom of the buttrock prices, then you won't ever get there." Amie said and smiled.

"Because the math doesn't work out," Casey stated, realizing that Amie had most likely gotten the same education in business math from Noah as he did.

"So the rate I charge now is the rate I need to run my business while doing the types of sessions I want to do. I simply thought about what that would be and I arrived at a number that made sense. I still want to be affordable enough for people that maybe don't have a huge income, but are treating their music as a serious hobby that helps them stay creative. But it's still high enough because I don't want to spend hours on people's stuff for peanuts. It costs too much to do something for very cheap because your opportunity cost is too high."

"Opportunity cost?" Casey asked.

"The time you waste working on something when you could be working on anything else."

"Is this back to business math?" Casey asked and rolled his eyes in jest. Noah laughed and interjected, "The opportunity cost of doing one activity for free instead of working on growing your business is just too great."

Amie expanded on the concept. "I look at my monthly budget and simply think: *ok, how many people will I need to work with to sustain that?* And every client that needs a discount needs to be weighed against another project that is paying full price."

"So you're never flexible on your prices?" Casey asked.

"Not at all. I still offer discounts to people, especially if I really love their work. I'm doing it for love after all. You know what I mean, right?"

Casey nodded, "Yeah it's definitely something I'd do for free if I could afford it."

"Right, and I think the price I'm at is a balance between being professional, which I am, but also being accessible. And I've always tried to walk that line."

"What about your early clients?" Noah asked Amie, grinning.

Amie chuckled, "Well... when the prices were lower, the clients were not as serious. I mean, no disrespect to the people I worked with in the early days. Some of them were absolutely incredible and I am grateful to have worked with those people. But some didn't have a lot of basic knowledge because they hadn't invested their time in it."

"Did those sessions suffer because of their lack of investment in themselves?" Noah asked.

"Absolutely. I realized that there was a strange correlation between price and professionalism. Those early clients weren't able to do that because they didn't understand and hadn't bothered to put in their own time to get to a level of quality that was needed to create a professional product."

"And how is it now?" Casey asked.

"99% of the artists I work with now are absolutely nailing it!" Amie exclaimed.

Noah swallowed a bite of pizza and said, "Casey, I brought you here to meet Amie because I wanted you to dive deeper into understanding your customer."

Casey prepared for the mental note-taking required whenever Noah started talking.

"First off, you won't be for everyone, so you need to make sure you qualify the clients that you want to work with. It is your decision whom you want to work with, and if you want to make an impact, you can only work with serious people that understand your value. The others aren't worth it because they'll make everything miserable."

"Right."

"And helping serious artists make an impact is

something that's not only worth a lot of money in the long run, once you become successful, but it's also personally enriching to yourself as you navigate the challenges of your career. Take Amie for example. How do you feel about your career having worked on so many different projects?"

"It's so much fun! Working on so many different projects all over the world is a feeling that's unlike any other," Amie said with a smile.

"And being able to find so many different projects all over the world, ironically, comes down to being very specific about who you want to work with. You have to really understand your ideal client."

"My ideal client?" Casey asked.

"As we said before, a client who's only looking to choose you based on your price isn't the type of person that's looking to create a relationship with you. They're trying to get a deal, and that's not really where you want to start the relationship. A client is nothing more than a friend you do business with." Noah let his words hang and Casey contemplated how quickly things turned sour with his first client. Not exactly friendship material.

"How well do you know your friends?" Noah asked Casey.

"I mean, pretty well, especially those I've been friends with forever."

"So, would you say you understand them pretty well?"

"I suppose so," Casey nodded.

"So when something is wrong, they may not even have to tell you because you can feel it. Is that a right assumption?" Noah asked.

"Absolutely, I can easily tell and it's easy for me to understand because we go way back."

"That's how I want you to understand your clients. All their hopes and dreams and pains and fears, so that you know instinctively what they need from you. When you have an early conversation with a client, you want to probe them about every little thing so that you can understand how to serve them in the best way possible. You want to understand your clients intimately."

Casey knew how much better his recording sessions went when he got more familiar with his clients' music and goals. He realized just how important this understanding was to create win-win situations in the studio.

"And more importantly, you want them to feel like you understand their problems. If you can explain the problem in such a way that they think that you understand their problem better than they actually understand it themselves, they are more likely to believe that you can help them overcome it—or that you're at least knowledgeable enough to be trustworthy to maybe take the next step together."

"And what should I be asking them?" Casey wanted to know.

"Anything that helps you understand how to help them better and make a bigger impact," Noah said, at which point Amie chimed in, "In my case, and it's pretty similar for you if you're doing recording projects. I would ask a lot of questions, like are the songs finished? Does everybody know how to play their parts or do you need to add pre-production in there? Are the musicians qualified and confident in their musicianship or will you need more time than usual to get a good performance?"

"I think I understand," Casey said. "These answers will help me gauge how much time the project is actually going to take, like how much time will recording take, or even worse, how much editing time will I need."

Amie laughed and nodded, "It puts everything into perspective and helps you understand what they're trying to achieve by hiring you. What is the vibe they're looking for? Who are their influences? What are they hoping the end result will sound like? Some musicians may not have thought about the possibilities in production because they've only played their music live. They will not have thought about overdubs, or additional instrumentation. They may not realize that if their song isn't 100% finished it will be hard to record in the studio."

"Not to mention expensive," Noah chimed in. "Just because you know what the session needs doesn't mean that they have any idea. You are the professional leading them through their recording journey. Even the most talented artists might be totally unaware of what's required to create a good production."

"If they don't know what they're expecting to get,

how am I supposed to charge a price in the face of such uncertainty?" Casey said.

"How would you estimate a price?" Amie asked.

Casey thought it over for a moment and said, "I suppose I'd estimate a certain amount of hours in the studio for recording each song, based on the instrumentation and the quality of their performance from any demos or live shows. Then I'd add a few hours of editing time and potentially a flat rate per song for mixing and mastering."

"What else?" Noah asked.

"I'd put together a proposal that listed a rate that included all those estimates, with a certain number of hours in the studio for recording the songs, with the understanding that if we were to go over those hours or anything out of the ordinary came up there would be a renegotiation of terms?" Casey finished his thoughts, uncertain about his ideas.

"Now you're getting it," Noah said.

"Asking questions and understanding what each party can expect from the other will make your business relationships smoother from the start," Amie added.

"When you make yourself a crucial member of the musical project, you become a leader of sorts. They're already coming to you for guidance because you are a mentor figure and they don't know how to do all this stuff. And when you help them see just how much of an impact their music will make when it's done correctly, without skimping on hours or costs, it'll light a fire under their butts because they'll want that! You've taken the time to understand everything about them so it's easy for them to see you as a part of that vision. Now it doesn't make sense for them to go with anybody else because that vision is just as much your creation as theirs. You're a critical part of it," Noah said.

The trio finished their lunch and parted ways. Casey's head was reeling from all of the knowledge they shared with him and he was excited to really dig into identifying his ideal client and whom he could help the most.

That week Casey focused on understanding his core customer. He interacted with musicians both online and off, trying to understand how they thought and what their motivations were.

He scoured online music communities, asked questions about what they were trying to achieve with their music and tried to infer their hopes and dreams. He knew that if he could understand their hopes and dreams, as well as their pains and fears, he could communicate his own value to them better, not only in the language that he used when talking to them, but also in the copy of his website and the messaging he would include in his marketing.

He understood the importance of speaking to his clients at their level, using the same language as they did. He started keeping a log of what the most common words other studios and music retailers would use to market to their customers, and scour any vocabulary his ideal clients would use so that he could understand their motivations and emotions when it came to the success of their music.

He tweaked his marketing copy so that it would be directed more towards what his ideal clients wanted to achieve instead of focusing on how great his studio and skills were. He also knew he could help potential clients with problems they had before they even needed him, so he put together a short series of videos that helped them overcome musical obstacles that he noticed were common inside many of the music communities he lurked in.

He answered questions with thoughtful answers and became active in many of the online communities where his clients hung out. He posted several short articles containing production tips with permission from the moderators and saw his website traffic increase as a result. Instead of constantly pestering bands to work with him through cold emails, he emailed valuable content to bands who joined his email list and started to create a relationship with them where he gave them value first, hoping to remain top of mind for whenever they needed his services down the line.

Now, whenever he got potential clients to his website, he had an easier time qualifying them because they chose their own adventure due to the way he structured his web pages. The people who weren't serious just read his articles and watched his videos. But the people who became his clients saw the value in hiring him because they understood the value and impact he brought to the table.

He created free content as a way to both market his expertise and to solve small problems he knew his audience could solve on their own. Instead of answering the same questions and wasting his valuable time, he could simply send those tire-kickers to his website to find the answer. That left him with more time to have serious conversations with artists that seemed interested in hiring him, while still maintaining good-will to those that might need him later down the road when they were ready.

SUCCESS STRATEGY #5
UNDERSTAND YOUR CUSTOMER
BETTER THAN THEY UNDERSTAND
THEMSELVES

Understanding the customer is to understand the people you are trying to serve. We are all customers in some shape or form. It's a part of being human. It's how we interact within the social construct of capitalism.

What are their hopes and dreams? People will justify their purchase with logic, but they will ultimately buy based on emotion. What is your customer hoping to achieve? How will they feel after going through your program, enlisting your services, or buying your product?

What are their pains and fears? You also need to know what they are trying to avoid. What is the emotional pain they are trying to eliminate? How do they talk about their problems in a negative way?

Customer demographics and geographics aren't enough anymore, especially for online businesses with a worldwide audience. You have to dig deeper and understand their interests, their worldview, and their lifestyle. Think about what they like and dislike to come up with your customer archetype.

Download the Customer Canvas worksheet to get
laser-focused on who your customer is at
www.YouGetWhatYouGiveBook.com

CHAPTER 12

WHICH PACKAGE WOULD YOU LIKE?

The following week Casey met Noah at yet another suave restaurant he picked out. This time it was a delicious Mexican restaurant known for its chimichangas and green corn tamales. The musicpreneur was chatting with the mariachi band when Casey arrived. Noah excitedly waved his arms to signal Casey to come over and join them. Casey wasn't much for mariachi, but he was curious about Noah's excitement.

"Casey, this is Sergio."

"Pleased to meet you," Casey said and shook Sergio's hand. The mariachi was impeccably dressed with a weathered nylon string acoustic guitar slung around his neck.

"Mucho gusto," the mustachioed mariachi said with a smile. Noah interrupted and said, "He's the leader of the best mariachi band in the city."

"Muchas gracias. We appreciate you saying that." A patron finished paying at the counter behind them and grabbed Sergio by the shoulder on the way out, gushing over their performance earlier, mentioning how much he liked their cover of "No Woman, No Cry," while handing him a $10 tip. Sergio graciously accepted his thanks and pocketed the tip.

"They are usually booked for months, and the restaurants fight for the best nights to book them when their schedule clears up," Noah explained.

"Wow, that's amazing. You guys must be really good," Casey said.

"Well, we really just know our audience and understand how to entertain our client's clients."

Entertain our client's clients, Casey thought.

"A rising tide floats all boats," Noah exclaimed.

"Sí, the mariachis make the margaritas overflow!" Sergio countered with a laugh. He leaned in closer and whispered, "These white people go absolutely crazy over our mariachi covers of pop songs. We just combined two genres to make something new the public wanted, and the bookings and tips flowed!" Sergio winked and gave a big belly laugh.

"That's innovation for you!" Noah exclaimed and laughed along with him.

Casey and Noah were whisked away by the server to a booth in the corner where Noah ordered their combination specialties for both of them.

"They must be raking in the dough if they're being fought over," Casey said.

"Yes, they've certainly increased their rates over the

years, but they bring in more value to the restaurants than what they charge, so the math works out."

"The business math, right. Always be thinking of how your work will help your client's success," Casey parroted from his previous lunches with Noah.

"Exactly. What you are learning now, Sergio learned a long time ago. Always think one step beyond just creating a relationship with your client. You want to be a valuable member of their team and focused on everyone's success," Noah said.

"I still feel stuck trying to increase my value. I'm not sure how I can break past the $100 session," Casey admitted with defeat in his eyes.

"Do you ever quote more than one price for your service?" Noah asked while slathering his tortilla chips with salsa.

"No? How can the same service have more than one price?" Casey asked back.

"A recent student ran into many of the same issues that you are experiencing now. He wanted to be a hip-hop producer and he loved making beats for rappers. And like you, he was constantly running into problems with starving artists who couldn't pay for his services."

"I know how he feels," Casey said.

"So he was having trouble making ends meet, but he realized that he could make a bigger impact by positioning himself differently. He was recording rappers for dirt cheap and it just wasn't working, so we dove into his business strategy and realized that the real impact he could make was to create different packages for different clients and focus on making his music work for him."

The last sentence piqued Casey's interest. "How did his music work *for him*?" Casey asked. "Did he stop recording?"

"No, he still did the occasional session, but it became just a small segment of his overall business model. He realized he could license his custom beats to all sorts of different clients—from small-time rappers to giant sound libraries."

"So he sold the same thing to different people?"

"In a way. He was a whiz at making cool arrangements, so whenever he had rappers come into the studio, he would quote three different packages. The first was the typical session if the rappers came in with their own productions, similar to what you're doing right now."

"Yeah, just pushing buttons and working on what's given to me," Casey nodded.

"Right, but then he offered higher-level packages that included the recording session, plus a non-exclusive license for a beat if they didn't have one already made."

"So he would create the music as well for a higher fee?"

"Not exactly. He would have productions lying around because he was so creative, so he always had a library of music he could demo for potential clients if they needed something new. It used to be that he would just include these beats in the recording session, but he realized that he could make more money by licensing them separately."

"And his clients took him up on that?" Casey asked.

"Some did, some couldn't. Some beats he offered with a non-exclusive license at a discount, which meant that he could use it again or send it off into a sound library to collect royalties. And some clients loved the idea of having a custom-built production that was exclusively for them so his third package was the deluxe VIP option he could charge a much higher premium for. And the more conversations he had with people, the better he became at qualifying the clients that he could serve the best.

"He understood whom he could serve the best because he took the time to understand their problems and their goals," Casey added.

"Exactly. It enabled him to be more involved in the process, which in turn made him happier and helped him make a bigger impact. He repackaged the beats, not as stand-alone products, but as added value with his more expensive services. He also qualified his customers better to see who were a better fit for his high-end services. Overall, fewer clients at a higher level made his career more manageable. And the best part was that anything he made that wasn't exclusive could be sent off to sample libraries or music publishers that specialized in selling his type of music to content creators and production houses that needed background music."

Casey's mind was racing with the possibilities of

creating different products at different levels depending on his client's needs. He felt a grumble in his stomach, and on cue the server arrived with their "very hot plates." They were filled to the brim with beans and rice, cheese enchiladas, green corn tamales, and shredded beef chimis. Noah's eyes widened and he dug in immediately, ignoring the server's warning about the hot plate.

"So, could I repackage what I do at different levels depending on what my clients are looking for?" Casey pondered aloud.

Swallowing a big bite, Noah said, "Yes, different packages at different levels, depending on your client's ability and willingness to pay for your services. Of course, you don't want to skimp on quality because at the end of the day you still want to put your name on the project, so your lowest price still needs to be the bare minimum you can charge to make a healthy profit. That's both best for you and your client."

"Right, lead with impact and don't skimp on quality," Casey said, his understanding of business coming together faster and faster.

"Positioning yourself in that way sets you apart. You're not racing to the bottom and trying to sell cheap services. You're no longer competing with those people anymore because you offer a more valuable service that's unique. Your offer isn't a commodity that feels single-serving and cheap. Yours is unique and personal, that adds the most value and impact you can bring to the table."

Casey understood his need to position himself apart from his competitors by offering something that was unique to his skills.

"That's how my beat making student transformed his failing business into a production powerhouse. Instead of competing in a bloody battle with the rest of the sharks in the ocean, he found a unique way to do business and created a blue ocean for himself."

Noah piled his fork full of rice and beans while chewing on his tamal.

"What's a blue ocean?" Casey asked and cut another piece of his enchilada.

"A blue ocean is when you have a unique value proposition that's different than what other people are offering. He's not competing with anyone because his offering stands apart from the competition. He's not a small fish in a big pond anymore. Hell, he's not even a big fish in a small pond. He basically has a monopoly on his own ocean!" Noah said and laughed.

"That way, he can command higher prices because his offer is unique. He still has the beats available as a package, but it's just a small addition to his income."

"Because he's also earning an income through his sample libraries?" Casey asked.

"Right, he has a diversified income stream, just like an investment portfolio. It spreads his income around and it also reduces his risk because no one client can be responsible for putting him out of business. There's always money coming in from somewhere else."

"Like Sergio's mariachi band," Casey said. "Each restaurant is an income stream."

"Right, and not only do they receive money from the restaurant for bringing in the customers, but they also receive tips and sell CDs at the front. Mind you, the CD sales don't count for much anymore, but there's always a certain demographic that buys them."

"So, they not only have a diversified income stream from their restaurant clients, but they also have multiple income streams inside each restaurant!" Casey exclaimed.

"You got it young padawan," Noah said and laughed. "Now, my student doesn't just sell beats and services like that anymore, but he's started creating courses on making beats that he sells, and he performs as a DJ as well, which only multiplies his income streams and increases his revenue overall."

"Selling courses?"

"Yes, for those who would like to learn how to do it themselves. He understands that not everyone wants to use his services, either because they can't afford it or they simply don't have the ability to do so. But the internet is a global place, so he's able to reach so many different people through his website, offering courses on beat making as well as sample packs and drum loops that he sells to them. It's become a big business machine, and he spends his days doing what he loves, working on music and helping other musicians make an impact with theirs."

Casey's eyes widened at the possibilities of creating

such a system for himself. The duo finished up their meals and margaritas and Casey set out to implement Noah's strategies for the week.

SUCCESS STRATEGY #6
DIVERSIFY YOUR INCOME

Just like you won't succeed in the stock market by betting on one stock, the same goes for your products and services. You should create as many income streams as possible because it'll safeguard you from failure. If you have multiple income streams and one dries up, it's not the end of the world. There's still money coming in from other places. Diversifying your income means you're taking your music career seriously and treating it like the business it is.

Diversifying isn't only limited to your money-making activities in such a black and white way. Diversification of your skill set can set you up to become much more valuable, not just to yourself, but to others that need a radically different skill set in the future that we are hurtling towards at an ever-increasing speed.

If you're looking for ideas on creating a diversified income and want to build a product suite that helps you make more money with less time, grab the worksheets at www.YouGetWhatYouGiveBook.com

CHAPTER 13
PUTTING IT TOGETHER

During the following week Casey worked on his website yet again, creating different services and packages that he could offer to potential clients. He didn't skimp on impact and quality, so everything he offered on top of his baseline services were things that could help his clients even further, while not negatively affecting the quality of their final product if they only selected his basic package.

He made his contact form ask qualifying questions so that he could know which clients would be worth going after and which ones were just looking for a cheap deal. He wrote multiple articles where he broke down every aspect of the production process and shared it with his growing audience. He wanted to convey how much better his client would be taken care of by him than by anybody else, so he shared his knowledge freely and set solid expectations from the start that not only helped him get better leads through his contact form, but also weeded out people that were only shopping on price.

He took responsibility for the outcome and results of his work, so any post-production that he assumed would be necessary was always rolled into the final price. Although he realized that it was up to the band to get the best performance, he knew that he would have to learn how to coax that performance out of them. It felt more transparent to Casey to set expectations based on their collective desire for results, instead of just quoting a price based on a random number of hours. Being honest and transparent about expectations from both parties created an easier working environment and trust between him and the artists he worked with.

He created a proposal system where he listed everything the artist would get when they booked with him: how many days in the studio they should expect for each song depending on the complexity, how many revisions they would have for each of their mixes, and he gave each prospective client a checklist of things they could do to prepare themselves for success in the studio. He offered this as a free download in exchange for musicians signing up to his email list and every day a few subscribers trickled in and reached out to him for more information.

Casey began to brainstorm all the different products and packages he could offer in the future but he left them in his folder for later because he knew better than to bite off more than he could chew at any one time.

His focus needed to be on working with artists and his website had to reflect his desire to do just that. *Later,* he thought. *After this first phase is over, I can focus on scaling up with new products and services.*

The next week Casey got a lead through his contact form. The email was from a girl called Alison who had written some songs she needed to record. Before, Casey would've just told her an hourly rate without thinking more about it, but this time he had Noah's wisdom on his side. He scheduled a meeting with her to explore how he could help her further.

When Alison showed up, she told him that she had recently moved to the city so she didn't know anybody and was looking to work on some songs she had written about her travels around the world. Casey was skeptical at first. She brought a banged up acoustic guitar and her chord fingerings were a little off. She seemed insecure about her songwriting, but when she started playing, Casey was floored. Her voice sounded amazing and the melody and lyrics wiped away any previous doubts he had. She finished her first song and sat on her stool awkwardly, fidgeting with her bracelets.

"Wow," Casey said, trying to hide his fluster. Alison's appearance had completely changed in his eyes, but he managed to stumble through his words and asked, "Do you have more songs like that?"

Alison shrugged and said, "I have about 30 that are finished and maybe another 20 that are works in progress… Do you think they are good enough to be recorded?"

"If they're anything like what you just played me, I would say so, yes!" Casey exclaimed, unable to hide his excitement and his love for a good song. Casey quickly put his producer hat on and decided that this was it. I'm not throwing away my shot, he thought and started asking Alison questions about her musical goals.

It turned out that Alison was somewhat of a vagabond, but was looking to settle down somewhere for a while. She was a location-independent freelancer, so she traveled from city to city with her guitar, working wherever she wanted and writing songs in between. She thought it was time to package her songs into something better than simple voice memos and sketches, and when she stumbled upon Casey's website, she had liked his obvious desire to help musicians make a big impact with their music.

"I'm glad I could get an introductory meeting with you to get a feel for if we could work together. I like your place," Alison said and waved her hand around his small home studio. "It's comfy."

"Thank you. Yeah, I can fit a whole band in here, although it's quite crowded when that happens," Casey said and laughed.

"So, do you think you can help me record a demo?" Alison asked.

Casey thought about offering her a simple acoustic guitar and vocal demo to start, but hesitated. This was bigger than that, and if he ever wanted to do sessions that become big, he had to think bigger than just a bare bones offering.

"You don't want to do a full production?" Casey asked back.

Alison seemed hesitant about investing in more than just an acoustic guitar and vocal demo, but Casey showed her some examples of what a production would do to a song. Luckily, he had some before/after examples and he showed her a sparse acoustic track that was pretty good when it sounded bare, just like her performance had, but when she heard the fully produced track with drums, supporting instruments, a rhythm section, and the whole nine yards she got really excited about the potential of her music.

He remembered Noah's words from one of his lunches, "Your job as a producer is to show them the potential their music can have. It's your job to imagine how their songs can sound. Make them imagine the instruments playing around them in the room, elevating their music to the next level."

As Casey's production example faded out, Alison asked wide-eyed, "And you can do all that?"

"I can play the instruments you can't play, and I can record and mix the entire record as well."

"Even the drums...?" Alison looked around the small room like she was looking for a place for the drums to sit.

"Actually, I've got something even better in mind for the drums," Casey said and smiled.

EPILOGUE
SOMEBODY LOAN ME A DIME

C asey knew a single song could change the world because he had lived it. A single song, a piece of music, a work of art, it all had the power to transform the future because it could affect the lives of people the same way a butterfly can create a tornado on the other side of the world.

Casey held the album cover of Boz Scaggs self-titled album as the "Loan Me a Dime" track came on his speakers. His living room was acoustically perfect, treated like a control room of a recording studio, but decorated by his wife Alison. He had listened to this song so many times that the record would skip in a perfectly looped section, the keyboard lick in the intro repeating itself perfectly. He'd always forget until the third or fourth skip through. He grinned as he stood up to help the needle into the next waveform.

The Swampers continued jamming their slow minor blues, a bendy blue-note guitar solo by the inimitable

Duane Allmann melancholically wailing before the haunting cries of Boz's vocals entered.

"If you haven't listened to this record late at night, the moonlight hitting your living room window and illuminating your second double scotch of the night, you haven't lived," Noah had told him a long time ago.

He held the record in high regard. He had two copies: one from his father with the characteristic skip he regularly played to himself. The second: a mint-condition edition from Noah.

Yes, he would forget until the third skip. Yes, he'd let it loop a few more bars for fun. No, he wouldn't replace the album with a new one.

His father would tell him the story of "Loan Me a Dime" in jest, but its meaning was astronomical. "We'd put on this record whenever we got bored by the girls we were hanging out with," he'd say. "They'd inevitably get bored of us making them listen to a thirteen-minute song that was mostly a guitar solo, so they'd want us to drop them off and we could go back out for the night."

The implications of this little story stuck with Casey his entire life because it was proof that a single song could alter the course of history. If it wasn't for that song, who knows whether he would have even been born? How many songs fluttered like butterflies into the ears of their listeners, changing their lives without them ever realizing?

This realization fundamentally changed his perspective on what mattered in life. It wasn't just trying to add as many zeroes to the bank account as possible. It wasn't about selling people a dream of what they could achieve. It was about finding the people who had the talents to change the world. In his case, he chose the changemakers of the music industry because music was fundamentally what drove him.

Every single moment of his life was tied to music in some way. A piece of music was a snapshot in time for the listener. A sonic memory that carried emotion, not just from the perspective of the writer and performer, but each listener would form their own emotional attachment based on what it meant to them. When an artist wrote a breakup song, the details surrounding the artist's breakup varied widely, but if they conveyed the emotion correctly, the song channeled a feeling through soundwaves that impacted the listener, causing a transfer of emotion that was undeniably powerful and unique to its artform.

Casey knew that the mind was malleable, and as long as he stuck to the routines and habits, his desired outcome became more likely. Being a successful creative had nothing to do with inspiration.

"Inspiration is a myth," Noah had told him. "Success is about hard work and dedication. Getting up every day and doing it again. Putting in the reps and working through the problems, not avoiding them. You can't find success waiting for it at some bus stop, like it's just going to roll up one day and you get on and pay your fare without any effort. Success comes from taking action and pushing yourself to become the person you want to be."

Noah had inspired Casey to take up his routines. Simplifying his decision-making reduced uncertainty and mitigated fear because he always knew what to do next. It was easy to get overwhelmed with big projects because he feared all the things that could go wrong, instead of focusing on all the ways they could go right. But he knew that if he'd let himself down that rabbit hole, days could go by without any meaningful progress.

"Get rid of as many distractions as possible to simplify your decisions," Noah had told him.

"The more complicated things become, the harder they are to manage. And inevitably you will find yourself at the point of diminishing marginal returns where the more you add, the worse you make it. Take the less is more approach and you'll end up with something that's greater than the sum of its parts. Make things simpler. Your success will come that much faster."

Casey knew that too many ingredients in a meal wouldn't make it taste better. Sometimes you just needed some salt, pepper, garlic and lemon juice. Taking something away could be even more effective than adding something extra.

Most songs worked with a strong foundation, a solid structure and a catchy melody. Once he learned the basics of business, it was just about repetition, finding what worked and doing it over and over again. Once he put the habits in place, developed the mindset to take action, and the willingness to fail along the way, nothing could stop him.

Looking back at his career was easy because the records lined the walls and the books filled the bookshelves. He chuckled at how naive he had been back then at Oasis Online Ops. How transformative a few lunches had been to set him on the path to become the successful person he was now. It was something that he had repaid the universe multiple times since then, paying it forward and serving others. Noah had made him promise to share the knowledge with as many people as he could. So he celebrated their wins every chance he got and gave others a forearm to hoist them up to the next level.

Casey heard a familiar melody coming from his speaker system and chuckled. He turned up The New Radicals and sat back in his chair. Michael Brauer's mix of "You Get What You Give" embraced his ears and the lyrics filled him with positivity.

SUCCESS STRATEGY #7
DEFINE YOUR SUCCESS

Before you go and put any of these lessons into action, you have to define what success looks like for you. At this time next year, in 12-months' time, how will your life look? Where do you want to be? Imagine that it already happened and work your way backward from there. What does successfully reaching your goal look like to you? Define the endpoint so that you have a goal post to work toward.

If you always keep moving the goalpost further down, you'll never feel like you've accomplished anything. To push forward, you have to move with a sense of accomplishment instead of a sense of insecurity. If you never allow yourself the chance to succeed because you keep moving the definition of success, you'll always feel like a failure.

Define what success means to you, make that success a habit and focus on the deep work you need to do in order to serve others.

If you've made it this far and want to continue further, I'd love to hear from you at
www.YouGetWhatYouGiveBook.com

THANK YOU

2.2 million books are published worldwide every year, so it feels like winning the lottery that you chose to read mine. I really hope that you enjoyed it, but more importantly, that it inspired you to make an impact with your own creative career.

Before you leave and put Noah's advice into action, I'd love to know what you thought. If you enjoyed the book please leave a review on Amazon or Goodreads to share your thoughts with others who may be interested in the book. That's honestly one of the best ways to share these lessons with others that might benefit.

ACKNOWLEDGEMENTS

When I started this book, we were in the "before times" where you could congregate at bars and go out to restaurants without worrying that you could catch a deadly disease that would kill your grandmother. To say that the walls have closed in since then is an understatement. As I finish this book, we are still in the beginning stages of the COVID-19 pandemic and uncertainty and anxiety are at an all-time high. Never before have I been as grateful for the friends and family that have kept me sane throughout this truly abysmal period of history. These are just a few of them who have supported me while writing this book, whether they knew it or not.

To my wife Liz and soon-to-be-daughter Lilja Sif, for always supporting me and quieting my insecurities when I really needed it. I love you and I can't wait for the world we're gonna make.

To my editor James Wasem, who looks at six thousand words of bullet points and sees a story. His early input and feedback were invaluable for making my ramblings into what you just read. And to the rest of the Audio Issues team, Kate Cannon and Jessica Sanchez, for all of their help keeping the business running and helping me make an impact in my students' lives.

To my dog Buckley, for having an uncanny understanding of when it's time to take a break and go for a walk.

A very special thanks to BLAMO, my weekly mastermind support group who have been with me for years through many a creative process. Lij Shaw, Matt Boudreau, Kevin Ward, Chris Selim, and Ian Shepherd: Here's my happy for this week.

Thank you to Emily Dolan Davies, Daniel Grimmett, Graham Cochrane, and Chris Graham for allowing me to interview them for a book that eventually got rejected, but its ideas turned into this one.

Thank you to my beta readers who took the time to give me helpful feedback for tightening up the story, especially John Walters, Alex Danvers, Tim Mann and Simon Rider. And special thanks to Sean Goslar for the heads up on the tamale ;)

To my Insiders community and Feedback Friday participants that continually surprise and inspire me with their creativity.

And finally, to my friends and family (and the Pod!) on both sides of the Atlantic. You have influenced me in more ways than you'll ever know.

ABOUT THE AUTHOR

Björgvin Benediktsson is an Icelandic-American author, audio educator, and entrepreneur. He is the founder of www.audio-issues.com where he has taught thousands of music producers how to make a bigger impact with their music since 2009.

He is the author of seven other books in the music industry, such as *Step By Step Mixing, Get More Gigs,* and *Better Mixes in Less Time.* He has written over 1,000 articles on music production and his advice has been featured in publications such as MusicTech magazine,

The Huffington Post, CD Baby's DIY Musician's Blog, Audiotuts, and the SAE Institute.

Björgvin is also an expert in online impact through authority building, thought leadership and email marketing. He's been studying online marketing and advertising since he enrolled in his uncle's online marketing school when he was 13 years old. He's coached companies on storytelling to win pitch competitions, given lectures on online marketing at universities, and mentored numerous companies and startups on customer development and online marketing throughout the years.

If you're looking for someone to help you create automatic email sequences that entertain your subscribers and turn them into buyers... if you're looking to understand your audience and customers better so you can create more products...or need an unlimited supply of content ideas to promote your business, Björgvin can help.

Made in the USA
Middletown, DE
26 December 2020

30148724R00102